STUDIES IN AFRICAN AMERICAN HISTORY AND CULTURE

Edited by
Graham Hodges
Colgate University

A ROUTLEDGE SERIES

Studies in African American History and Culture

Graham Hodges, *General Editor*

WOMANISM, LITERATURE, AND THE TRANSFORMATION OF THE BLACK COMMUNITY, 1965-1980

Kalenda C. Eaton

Routledge
Taylor & Francis Group
New York   London

First published 2008
by Routledge
270 Madison Ave, New York, NY 10016

0132584103

Simultaneously published in the UK
by Routledge
2 Park Square, Milton Park, Abingdon, Oxon OX14 4RN

Routledge is an imprint of the Taylor & Francis Group, an informa business

© 2008 Taylor & Francis

Typeset in Sabon by IBT Global
Printed and bound in the United States of America on acid-free paper by IBT Global

Library of Congress Cataloging in Publication Data
Eaton, Kalenda C.
Womanism, literature, and the transformation of the Black community, 1965–1980 / by Kalenda C. Eaton.
p. cm. — (Studies in African American history and culture)
Includes bibliographical references and index.
ISBN 0-415-96129-7
1. American fiction—African American authors—History and criticism. 2. American fiction—Women authors—History and criticism. 3. American fiction—20th century—History and criticism. 4. African American women authors—Political and social views. 5. Womanism in literature. 6. African Americans in literature. 7. African Americans—Race identity. 8. African Americans--Social conditions. I. Title.

PS374.N4E37 2007
813.009'928708996073—dc22

2007020476

ISBN10: 0-415-96129-7 (hbk)
ISBN10: 0-203-93590-X (ebk)

ISBN13: 978-0-415-96129-5 (hbk)
ISBN13: 978-0-203-93590-3 (ebk)

For the next wave

Yasmine
Morgan
Breana
Caché
Jada
Jayme
Jaysen
Germayne
Kelsey
Angelica
Angelia
Leigh
Chloe
Kristen

Contents

Preface: "Lifewriting"

For most of my life I have been convinced that my physical body was born a decade later than my soul. I have often been called an "old soul," by my elders, and have come to appreciate the term, but with that appreciation comes a feeling of displacement. My earliest memories involve a fierce understanding of my position in the world as a Black person and the power associated with that identity. Many would consider these sentiments more in line with a generation of Black youth who came of age in the 1960s rather than the early 1980s—but as I stated, I believe there was a slight mix-up in the drawing room. Or maybe not.

When I was born, my mother had only recently returned home after spending four life changing years as a college student on the other side of the nation. Her decision to step out on faith and pursue her dream of attending Howard University in Washington, D.C. simply because it was a premier Historically Black University has stood as a testament to the conviction I associate with pride in one's heritage. What she brought home from her journey was both tangible and intangible, and has served me in intimate and complex ways. I remember conversations we had in the lower level of my grandparents' house, a place where my mother would tell me that I was beautiful and that I came from beautiful people. I remember being instructed to ball up my little fist and pump it in the air while softly saying, then shouting "I'm Black and I'm proud, and I'll shout it out loud." I remember this.

As I got older the conservative backlash of the 1980s claimed the views and convictions of the "quiet revolutionaries" like my mother. She sacrificed our private affirmations in order to climb the corporate ladder and take care of us, only to find out the historical truth that Black, female, and educated meant enduring harassment, occasional jokes about "watermelons" at the office party, as well as physical and emotional stress. During this period, I devoured books. I read assigned homework, "Tween" literature ordered from the book catalogs at school, and detective books from the public library, all without pause. There was no match for my voracity. I ran through the texts like water, always left wanting more.

One day while sitting in our living room trying to entertain myself, I walked to the bookcase I had passed hundreds of times before. I silently read the titles: *The Bluest Eye, Sula, Song of Solomon, Another Country, Uncle Tom's Children, The Black Book, Native Son, If He Hollers Let Him Go* . . . There was also an anthology of "Negro" literature which included poetry by young artists like Giovanni, Sanchez, Baraka, and others. I had never read any literature by these writers, and wanted to know who they were. These were books acquired by my mother in college, some for classes she took, and others were purchased because of the "message." I started with the anthology and was immediately drawn into the beauty of the language. The words that described me, my family, and my community filled me with emotion. From that point on, my tastes matured. By the time I graduated from elementary school, I had read most of the books on the shelf. The more I read the more aligned with my thoughts, feelings, and convictions I became. Something inside clicked and immediately my soul shouted "hallelujah," and busily began preparing me for the future.

Though I appreciated all of the texts, I was particularly drawn to the depth and range of characters included in works by Black women. I recognized a more holistic representation of the Black community, long before I encountered Alice Walker's Womanist standpoint in college. I was intrigued by the depiction of ancillary characters whose placement in the novels comprised the foundation of the text. There was also a commonality of experience that I recognized. Though each plot was different, the "folk" in Zora Neale Hurston's novels reminded me of the folk in Morrison's fiction. Themes of beauty and pride in Black Arts Movement poetry was also present in Harlem Renaissance-era writing as well. Although I was a California child, the women looked like women I knew, the elders reasoned like my grandparents, etc. Not until I was much older did I consider the purpose beneath the images and dialogue.

At some point, I began to ask myself what it was about certain novels that I appreciated over others. It did not take long for me to identify those works infused with political discourse, as the stand out pieces. I have been interested in political mobilization, community organizing, and the revolutionary rhetoric associated with the 1960s and 1970s for nearly two decades. Therefore, I am intrigued by those Black women authors who went against the grain and published fiction (rather than poetry, autobiography, drama, or essays) during the post-Civil Rights period. What were their works able to convey? Were the authors and their characters speaking to the contemporary Black community? How did the dialogue reflect the complexity of the era? Were solutions to the dilemmas faced by the Black community included in the texts? These are all questions this book project attempts to explore.

The analysis that frames this project is based on my understanding of the needs that continue to plague the larger Black community. Although significant progress has been made over the past fifty years, there remains a considerable lack of parity between racial groups in the United States. It is no coincidence that the same rights and privileges fought for three decades ago remain highly debated in the 21st century. Likewise, "leaders" within the Black community (academics, politicians, entertainers) are sitting down at the table trying to determine the next course of action to combat the growing numbers of "lost" Black boys, and disillusioned young girls. In 2006, people are asking the same question activists and scholars asked in 1968: "Where do we go from here?" I was drawn to this project because the authors included present responses to that very question. For them, the answer lies within collective political action, the pooling of economic resources, the repatriation of a flighty Black middle class, and the re-affirmation of the Black community's value.

I have often lamented growing up in the San Francisco Bay Area, a decade after the pulse of the Black Panthers could be felt in the streets, but I know now that a certain amount of distance is often necessary for critical analysis. My scholarly contribution to the incessant challenges faced by the Black community help me to believe I did in fact come at the right time.

Acknowledgments

There are several people, places, and institutions that have contributed to the composition of this book. I am not able to include everyone, but I publicly thank the following in this order: My maternal and paternal grandmothers for living their lives according to their own rules, and warning me against taking myself too seriously; my maternal grandfather for daring to survive against the odds and making sure that I understood the importance of my "lesson;" my mother Linda Eaton Young, for her unconditional love, support, and foresight—you lead by example; my fathers for their wisdom and encouragement; my uncles and aunts who are individual examples of grace, wisdom, and love; and my cousins who cleared the path, make me laugh, and teach me how to live. All of my teachers, formal and informal, who took the time to nurture my passion for learning. Some of my mentors include: Dorothy Walker, Maralyn Scott, MJ Punche, Chandra Mountain, Elizabeth Marsden, Rudolph Byrd, Cynthia Spence, Jacqueline Jones Royster, Beverly Moss, Debra Moddelmogg, Oyekan Owomoyela, Helen Connell, Karen Callaghan, Barbara DiBernard, and Maureen Honey. Thank you Valerie Lee, for your continued support of my dreams. My sisters and sister-friends: Regina, Karen, Jonuell, Nichole, Tara, Aisha, Esther, Nicole, Jeannette, Sumalee, and Trimiko. A special thank you to my husband, Randell R. Donald, for his encouragement, support, love, advice, patience, and calming spirit. Thank you for your willingness to "make it happen," wherever my dreams take you. You are always spiritually grounded and eager to live each day to the fullest. I am constantly motivated by your self-determination. Congratulations on your album. I thank the MMUF program for its support and for enhancing the Academy with our presence.

Chapter One
"Let Me Know When You Get Through"
The Afro-Politico Womanist Agenda

Don't you know? They're talkin' bout a revolution—it sounds like a whisper
Don't you know? They're talkin' bout a revolution—it sounds like a whisper
Finally the tables are starting to turn, (talkin' bout a revolution)
'Cause finally the tables are starting to turn, (talkin' bout a revolu-tion) . . .

—Tracy Chapman (1988)

Several Black feminist critics have examined female subjugation and the alleged exclusion of Black women's voices during the "Black Power Move-ment," and/or the years that fall between 1966–1976. Scholars including Patricia Hill Collins, Madhu Dubey, bell hooks, Angela Davis, Barbara Christian, and Joy James, are a few who represent a wide range of theoretical scholarship on the role of the Black woman in the variegated "community."[1] Significantly, it is argued that these years represent the reclamation of the black community by virile, "masculine warriors" (i.e., Black men), through organizational leadership and community organizing. As is commonly stated, during this period the Black political platform became a predominantly mas-culinist one, and not surprisingly, the fight against racial oppression ignored internal gender oppression within the black community.

In addition, this earlier Black feminist critique of black masculine ide-ologies notes that while increased male participation and persuasive rheto-ric identifying the black man as "king" increased notoriety and garnered mass support for various organizations, the success was contingent upon female subjugation. Here Michelle Wallace's seminal *Black Macho and the Myth of the Superwoman* (1978) is key as she interrogates the role of

1

black women in the folds of exclusively masculine rhetoric and misogynistic underpinnings. She identifies black women's initial reluctance to speak against the performance of "macho," as a fear of being deemed "counterrevolutionary"—which was assumed to ultimately lead to the destruction of the black family. Accordingly, the mythical "Strong Black Woman," who exists through a rejection of male domination and systematic gender oppression, is deemed a detriment to the progress of the Black community because of her overbearing demeanor and emasculating tendencies.

Though Wallace has been derided for statements that argue "rampant misogyny" exists within the community, and she has modified her position somewhat in recent years, the premise behind *Black Macho* is equally important as the criticism it aroused. Among other topics, Wallace argues that, unlike Black female abolitionists, Black "Club Women" at the turn of the 20th century, or Black feminists who preceded the 1960s—women during the Black Power movement were not "allowed" to do anything important (Wallace 162). Because "there was more parading of Black macho than revolutionary planning" the silencing and subsequent absence of women meant the fall of the Movement (78–81). In contemporary scholarship, while the popular attention is on the rhetoric of the era and the prevalence of a Black masculine discourse based on the reclamation of power, understanding these truths does not constitute a comprehensive portrait of Black women's activity during the era.

Like the *strong* Black woman, the mythic *silent* Black woman has often been misread and idealized during the height of the Black revolutionary period. She is seen as a quiet and willing supporter, working for the cause but (except for a few cases), not in the forefront of activism. For example, in Pratihba Parmar's documentary "A Place of Rage," June Jordan acknowledges that many Black women felt guilty for "contributing" to an alleged matriarchal domination that emasculated Black men, and in turn dutifully accepted their places "ten steps behind" their leaders (Parmar *Rage*). What most historical studies of the era fail to acknowledge is the brevity of this passive position, and the diligent social and political activity led by women in grass-roots organizations, including the artistic work of black women novelists. The focused organizing within the Black community was a useful and necessary undercurrent to the self-aggrandizement and political rhetoric which became an unwelcome distraction to complex internal issues.

Generally, during this period in Black political history the community at-large appeared to exhibit disillusioned and nihilistic attitudes toward an uncertain future—a reaction that ultimately led to a rupture in indigenous organizational strength. In *Political Process and the Development of Black*

Insurgency, 1930–1970, Doug McAdam responds to urban uprisings in the late 1960s as the result of an alleged void in organizational leadership and failed community organizing. He argues:

> If the riots of this period conveyed an image of escalating racial conflict, they also masked a series of more subtle processes that were simultaneously at work undermining the efforts of insurgents to develop the organizational and tactical forms needed to sustain the leverage attained by the movement during the mid-1960s. The result of these processes was dramatic and quickly felt. By 1970, the movement, as a force capable of generating and sustaining organized insurgency, was moribund, if not dead (McAdam 182).

Admittedly, by 1970 the Black community appeared to rest at a dangerous crossroads that reflected Martin Luther King's timeless question, *Where Do We Go From Here: Chaos or Community?* (1968). The assassinations and losses of King, Malcolm X, Patrice Lumumba, Fannie Lou Hamer, John F. Kennedy, *et al.* and the banning of the African National Congress in South Africa produced a heightened social and political consciousness among Black people worldwide. There were no answers to the failure of white hegemony to recognize and respect the political rights of people of color. The ability of the American corporate structure to evade important legislation like the Civil Rights Act (1964), the Equal Employment Opportunity Act (1965), and the Fair Housing Act (1968) evidently supported the argument that "discrimination in employment and in the housing market continue[d] to prevail" (Bell 7).

The chaos and confusion that existed resulted from the fallacy of racial integration and social improvements for Black America. In addition to a scorched social landscape, prominent leaders in Black Power movement organizations were in exile, imprisoned, or strategizing within an academic atmosphere. Older movement veterans appeared to quietly back away from the national spotlight and associated themselves with local fights and struggles still brewing in their home communities. The Northern ghettoes began to worsen and in many ways outdo the rural South in terms of poverty, economic degradation, poor living conditions, and lack of access to quality education (King 35). Likewise, large numbers of the Black Middle class were beginning the deft escape to a suburban, conservative way of life that the Civil Rights Movement made possible.

Given the reality of the 1960s as a decade of Black death and disillusionment for many, the commonly criticized raised voices of "angry" Black youth inaccurately account for a decline in sustained political organization within the Black community—especially since many global struggles were just beginning to take shape. What McAdam and other scholars identify as the "end" of the Civil Rights Movement was actually a respite for many who had sacrificed non-stop and ridden the wave of social change and Black frustration. Although the years 1970–1980 represent a shift in Black politics from the radicalism of the mid to late 1960s to a more fragmented approach to Civil Rights and injustice, it can be argued that Black activism continued to grow and expand through a less cohesive process. One method of categorizing the confused state of the Black community connects its fractured organizational structure with the rise of a postmodern understanding of social constructs and rejection of traditional unified goals. Terry Eagleton defines postmodern angst and skepticism in the following way:

> . . . [S]uspicious of classical notions of truth, reason, identity and objectivity, of the idea of universal progress or emancipation, of single frameworks, grand narratives or ultimate grounds of explanation. . . . [It] sees the world as contingent, ungrounded, diverse, unstable, indeterminate, as set of disunified cultures or interpretations which breed a degree of skepticism about the objectivity of truth, history and norms, the givenness of natures and the coherence of identities" (Eagleton vii).

As the social climate shifted from an embrace and acceptance of Black unity and African heritage, Postmodernism as an innovative method of understanding social processes worked to eliminate the fundamental basis of the Civil Rights Movement. The concept of collective action and organizational strength appeared unable to survive within the context of instability and indeterminacy that marked the 1970s. Ironically, though Postmodernism is a definite source of the rejection of collective history and a shared cultural vision for the future, the terms "postmodern" and "blackness" have a love/hate relationship within Black scholarship. Although Postmodernism is born out of a decade of civil rights action and open defiance of previously established racial and social norms, postmodern scholarship has traditionally ignored its ties to the fight for racial equality and the redefinition of the nation-state.

This simultaneous inclusion and exclusion of Black experience has led to Black scholars denouncing Postmodernism as a white theoretical concept that cannot accurately define Black experience. In the article, "Postmodern Blackness: Toni Morrison's *Beloved* and the end of history," Kimberly Chabot Davis contends, " . . . we should be [wary] of concluding that postmodernism is a "white" phenomenon. Any claim that the lives of black people have nothing to do with postmodernism ignores the complex historical interrelationship of black protest and liberal academic discourse" (Davis 2). Davis recognizes the dependent relationship between the advent of a postmodern world and the socio-political conditions that fueled the global revolts of the 1960's. As a result of social uprisings (led by the Civil Rights Movement) and critical analyses on the demise of modernism, cultural politics and the indeterminacy of political action *were* more readily explored. An unfortunate opportunity cost of this "progressive" era was a cohesive struggle for Black political progress. With the rejection of established cultural norms and traditions, disunity among leaders of the Black community reflected the impending future.

Accordingly, as a "new," "young," and "militant" leg of the Civil Rights movement gained popularity the collaborative community organizations that existed before were ultimately pitted against each other in an attempt to initiate self-destruction. For example, those groups that considered themselves Revolutionary Nationalists openly rejected the aims of Cultural Nationalism claiming the latter to be "pork chop" nationalism, reactionary nationalism, and accused Cultural Nationalist leaders of conspiring with the despised "pig" (the "white" justice system and racist police officers). Likewise, cultural nationalists ridiculed "so-called revolutionaries" for hiding behind anarchist rhetoric that did nothing to aid Black progress.

Not surprisingly, the political infighting and breakdown of community-based coalitions was not lost on Black women authors. For example, in *The Salt Eaters* by Toni Cade Bambara, one of the characters comments on divergent communal goals and the gradual adoption of alternate paths for liberation stating, "I dunno. Malcolm gone, King gone, Fanni Lou gone (sic), Angela quiet, the movement splintered, enclaves unconnected. Everybody off into the Maharaji This and the Right Reverend That. If it isn't some far-off religious nuttery, it's some otherworldly stuff" (Bambara 193). Though the political outcome appeared bleak for the Black community and the adoption of ways outside the traditional reference points of Black experience were encouraged by the changing socio-political landscape, this restless and chaotic period in the continuum of Black political experience was the calm before the storm for Black female activists and authors. Placing emphasis on the incapability of sustained "organized insurgency" after 1970, neglects an examination of viable, on-going community activism in the writings of Black women activists and writers. Authors were able to view social movements as "discursive fields of action" that did "not always look like a movement or function "as the way movements have been defined" (Alvarez). Through a comprehensive examination of the changing worldscape, Bambara and others challenge traditional understandings of political mobilization and activism while using spirituality to discuss power and economic stability. Her visionary work comes forward in a space designed to complement the multifaceted political experiences of Black women in the African Diaspora.

This "revolutionary" period also saw the rise of what is commonly regarded as Black feminist theory within the global public and political sphere. The movement, organization, and attention of Black women aggressively regained its position as the true vanguard of Black community activism. Likewise, diverse representatives of Black womanhood regained credibility after being embraced by the new Black scholarly elite. Robin Kelley asserts that:

> The radical black feminist movement, not unlike other feminists, also redefined the source of theory. It expanded the definition of who constitutes a theorist, the voice of authority speaking for black women, to include poets, blues singers, storytellers, painters, mothers, preachers, and teachers. Black women artists are often embraced from all parts of the diaspora . . .

> . . . [R]adical black feminism offers one of the most comprehensive visions of freedom I can think of, one that recognizes the deep interconnectedness of struggles around race, gender, sexuality, culture, class, and spirituality (Kelley 154).

What Kelley observes is the ability of creative artists, musicians, and storytellers to resist the postmodern focus on indeterminacy and severed communal relationships. Through their everyday, continued efforts to ensure health and stability within the Black community, Black women restored hope and kept possibilities for a positive future ever-present.

Like Kelley's observation above, this project is concerned with an inclusive analysis of the overall socio-political structure of the black community during the "revolutionary" years (1965–1980). It is aware that behind the scenes, significant revolutionary activity was taking place. Black women activists were working within and writing about the Black community in ways that they hoped would ensure progressive action after the signing of Civil Rights legislation and in the coming years. A few examples of this continued work include: Ella Baker's activism through organization-centered politics, Fannie Lou Hamer's local and national activism on behalf of the poor and working class, as well as the emergence of literature written by Black female novelists who made conscious decisions to tell the stories of those most affected by social upheaval and racial tensions in the American South.

As a means of dealing with the pervasive problems within Black organizational leadership, these women employed what I call "let me know when you get through" approach. I take this from a sarcastic colloquial expression that exists in the Black American vernacular tradition, typically used at meetings or large gatherings where discussion of a subject "gets out of hand," and no progress is being made. For example, "Let me know when you get through arguing about [the issue]. I'll be over here." The tone of the phrasing suggests that time is being wasted while individuals debate irrelevant and useless themes. When the person who initiates the statement moves to the side, her self-removal is not a sign of retreat, but a sign to those addressed that she is serious about the work at hand and that their actions are bordering on foolishness. This expression as strategy signifies on the Black revolutionary movement itself by showing that the continued emphasis on distinctions between Black Nationalist ideologies, for example, were distractions from pragmatic issues and problems the black community faced. While the leaders continued to argue over the correct philosophical path for Black progress, Black women activists and writers were "over [t]here" working within their communities to ensure progress would be made. Instead of furthering arguments by Black leaders that one method of political action was/is more successful than another, select Black women writers address the endless possibilities for the Black community if both Black cultural pride *and* an emphasis on political revolution were to merge harmoniously.

THEORETICAL FRAMEWORK: AFRO-POLITICO WOMANISM

Community-based activism during the Civil Rights Movement and beyond laid the groundwork for several modes of theoretical scholarship regarding the "Black woman." Black Feminist Theory, Womanism, Africana Womanism, and Womanist Theology are examples of scholarship that received critical attention in the post-Civil Rights era. Each term argues for a specific theoretical framework. Examples of their respective foci include: the enhancement of traditional "white feminism" to include the voices of women of color; an exclusive emphasis on race, class, and gender; understanding the experiences of Black women as part of the African Diaspora; the position of women within the Black church (and) as part of spiritual and religious movements.

While a positive argument can be made for the use of each approach listed above, this project relies on what I call an "Afro-Politico Womanist" (APW) agenda—an inclusive and progressive theoretical approach to literary activism as it relates to an ideological understanding of the Black community. As a combination of Black Feminism and Womanism, the Afro-Politico Womanist framework incorporates Black female activism, History, Literature, and Experiential Theory into the reading of texts. The emphasis in this model is a holistic, community based approach to political mobilization within the Black community which was largely ignored during the activism of the post-Civil Rights period.

The framework prioritizes the strength, survival, unity, and health (mental and physical) of the global black community, by first, addressing the needs and concerns of the existing poor and working class, as they define these needs. Afro-Politico Womanism resists reliance on singular leadership as the method by which members of the Black community understand their roles in the political process. The concept supports portions of Alice Walker's definition of "Womanism,"[2] specifically, the phrase "committed to the survival and wholeness of an entire people, male and female."

APW is committed to positive literary representations of Black female political activism, and often exists in 20th century literature written by black women, in which the protagonist(s) has a strong desire to "disrupt the infrastructure." In the context of this project, literary representations of Black female political activism includes a character's struggle for justice within the Black community and an understanding of how healthy gender relationships can be used to heal the Black community. Black authors whose work falls under this definition write within the socio-political context of insurgency or transformation in the "imagined" Black community. The female characters act as agents in an effort to expose inaction (or perilous action) of the American polity. Instead of focusing solely on gender oppression and gendered violence within the black community, I argue that Black female artists engaged in a fight for common goals, while at the same time acknowledging the usefulness of a woman-centered theoretical model.

As with any innovative theoretical approach or framework certain justifications must be made, and questions answered. For example, possible questions concerning APW are "Can any Black woman be read according to the APW paradigm?" "Or, "Have not Black women been characterized this way for years? What makes Afro-Politico Womanism different?" The purpose of defining another model is not to emphasize difference, but to address the work of a specific type of organizer and activist who exists within Black literature and is traditionally ignored in historical and political reflections on the Black revolution. By using literature as a form of

activism, the Black woman writer's insider position and stake in the eradi-
cation of injustice enables her to negotiate multidimensional experiences
(i.e. Black/woman/partner/writer/activist). For women fighting against sub-
alternity, writing and political activism are not mutually exclusive.

Obviously, in Black literature, not all works that have female protagonists central to the theme of the text follow the direction of the Afro-
politico Womanist agenda. Within the parameters of this paradigm, several
literary works otherwise popular for their "strong black female" or "Black
feminist" perspective are ultimately unable to fulfill the agenda's goals. For
example, these works may include protagonists who exist apart from the
community and devalue political mobilization and/or when faced with a
choice the characters may choose individualism over action on behalf of
the larger community. Two examples of literary characters who counter
the goals of Afro-Politico Womanism are Lutie Johnson in Ann Petry's
The Street (1946), and Janie Starks in Zora Neale Hurston's *Their Eyes
Were Watching God* (1937). While these works are major contributions to
the Black female literary canon, the characters associate with others on a
superficial and guarded level, and exist as their male counterparts—without vested interest in the Black community.

With Lutie Johnson, after battling the streets of Harlem and confront-
ing the estrangement of her husband, she is sexually harassed and attacked
by an unscrupulous benefactor. Lutie decides that she can only reclaim herself and her personal strength through self-erasure. Contrary to the collective power of minority groups, as an individual, Lutie believes her race
and gender leave her powerless. After realizing she has no influence on the
political structure, she risks everything, including her son, and murders
her attacker. Her final act of defiance—flight—casts her as one among the
nameless and faceless multitude.

Curiously, as a fugitive from the law, Johnson then becomes a fugitive from her "maternal role," which increases the threat of capture and
imprisonment. Ultimately, she chooses to be alone, an act associated with
male dominance and freedom. She remains disconnected from all ties to
family and community, and becomes like the outlaw hero of the American western. According to Robert Ray, the outlaw hero regards the law
"as a collective, impersonal ideology imposed on the individual from without . . . generat[ing] a rich tradition of legends celebrating legal defiance
in the name of some "natural" standard . . . " (Ray 312). Lutie's belief
in her *natural* right to independence and the American Dream defies the
restrictions placed on her as a poor Black woman.

Another useful example of the perils of individualism is the "disruptive" figure of Janie Starks (neé Crawford), the protagonist of Zora Neale

Hurston's *Their Eyes Were Watching God*. Janie moves from dependency to autonomy in her refusal to accept social strictures. Janie is born into a perpetual cycle of peonage, which her grandmother, Nanny, intends to break, first through hopes of education and ultimately through an arranged marriage. As the reader learns, Janie's grandmother sees assimilation into the elite classes of African Americans as the only real solution to Janie's perilous position as "de mule uh de world."

Later in the novel, after two "failed" marriages to upwardly mobile black men (Logan Killicks and Joe Starks), Janie enters into a controversial relationship with Teacake, a young, "free spirit," belonging to the lumpen class of Southern blacks. Janie's subsequent decision to shoot Teacake (when he is stricken with rabies) and the trial that follows, places her in the heart of "one of the most controversial and hotly contested aspects of the novel: whether or not Janie is able to achieve her voice . . . " (Washington xi). In actuality, Janie is placed on trial by the Black community for being a member of the elite class, rather than the euthanasic death of Teacake.

When Janie rejects Killicks, whom her grandmother identifies as "a good man," she rejects complacency and traditional gender roles—Janie as cook, maid, and mother. She is initially attracted to Joe Starks' rhetoric and his leadership ability, but soon finds his emphasis on upward mobility, a "woman's place," and their separation from the Black lower classes oppressive. Therefore, her relationship with Teacake is viewed as wild and adventurous from her point of view, but fraudulent by the masses. In the end, Janie gains approval on the witness stand from the white all-male members of the jury and the group of upper class white women who "wore good clothes and had the pinky color that comes with good food"(176). Because Janie refuses to speak and/or acknowledge her privileged class position, the black community in the courtroom views her with contempt. Because she identifies herself as one of the folk, though she is not, the members of the indigenous class shun her for her apparent mockery of their speech, actions, and dress. As a result, they read her as an agent of white oppression. She further supports this accusation by rejecting noninstitutionalized tactics[3] and abandoning the environment once she is acquitted.

I use these two examples to show that although the literary texts are otherwise powerful statements of Black women's ability to resist the holds of racial and gender oppression, when considering the larger picture, Lutie and Janie are not heroes. They serve as examples of those who are "radical," "revolutionary," and "political" in the context of shifting the focus from the greater good to personal gain and survival while transgressing traditional feminine roles. While this standpoint can be empowering, it has damaging and unhealthy effects on the scope of community development and activism. The women highlighted represent the marginal position of the Black feminist when *separated* from the Black collective. Therefore, their desire to achieve freedom through autonomy places them outside the parameters of a Womanist standpoint.

As stated previously, APW is created out of the existing needs of the community. Under this model, individualism is closely aligned with flaws in organizational leadership, and is viewed as counter-productive to attempts at collective growth and racial progress. Because literary representations of women like Janie and Lutie show them as peripheral to the community, they cannot exist under the *Afro-Politico Womanist* paradigm—a model whose success is based on work within and for the immediate community. As outlined above, APW does not readily apply to all works traditionally viewed as instrumental to an understanding of Black womanhood. Fictional female characters and real world activism assessed according to this paradigm privilege a collective healing that shifts the focus from what literary scholar Valerie Lee terms a "solitary posture of the protagonist" to an extrinsic focus on the plight of the Black community.

AFRO-POLITICO WOMANIST FICTION[4]

As stated previously, my project is situated between 1965–1980, as a way of pinpointing a key era in the ongoing fight for racial and social justice and the emergence of Womanism and Black Feminist theory. The space between the Civil Rights Movement and the ultra-conservative Reagan era is not only regarded as the era of Postmodernism, but also a period of intra-national debate on gender politics and racial equality. Likewise, 1966 marks the year Stokely Carmichael ushered the term "Black Power" into American consciousness and the second wave of the mainstream feminist movement gained national recognition. In the respective works outlined in the following chapters, the authors have created characters that exist outside of the political and material gains of the accomodationist model, as well as the vigilantism associated with revolutionary rhetoric.

In the fictional work of Toni Morrison, Alice Walker, Toni Cade Bambara, and Paule Marshall, the Black community as a nation separate and culturally specific is naturally defined within the scope of black women's experiences. In a move toward inclusion and creative protest, their writings cover a wide range of Black men and women's experiences which are reified and made available for public consumption. The authors in this study employ the simultaneous ability to critique, love, destroy, and create representations of the Black family, Black love, Black thought, and Black experience used to preserve the principles of Black Nationalism and community-based political action. According to this model, what certain Black male critics later define as "airing dirty laundry"—is actually an act of liberation by these female writer-activists.

The first novel, Toni Morrison's *Song of Solomon* (1977), is a cautionary novel that warns of the impending destruction of the community if ideological battles continue to shift the focus away from the pulse of the Black community. In Chapter Two I discuss the work in the context of Black Nationalism, paying specific attention to the manifestations of Revolutionary and Cultural Nationalism within Black culture. I use Afro-Politico Womanism to critique Black Nationalist rhetoric and ideology that excludes alternative ways of imagining community progress. This critique identifies racial integration, organizational dissonance, and the emergence of a politically divided Black middle class as a precursor to structural demise of the Black community.

I read Morrison's primary characters, Milkman Dead and Guitar Baines, as symbolic of cultural and revolutionary nationalist ideology. Though both young men serve as symbols of a hopeful future within a community of elders, their oppositional politics (Milkman as child of the Black Aesthetic, and Guitar as proponent of Black Militancy) threaten the sanctity of a community that needs the talents of both men to survive.

Alice Walker's *Meridian* (1976), often defined as a "Civil Rights Movement novel," serves as a portal through which the type of activism that privileges both Cultural and Revolutionary Nationalism can emerge. In Chapter Three, I read the characters Meridian Hill and Truman Held as contrasting figures who understand the imperative of relationship building as connected to the pursuit of a sanctified and whole Black community— whether or not the community is willing to act on its own behalf. Meridian continues grass roots political mobilization in small Southern communities that serve as the basis for her life of activism and leadership, while Truman wanders as a prodigal son of the South, until realizing that the key to his future is the return of the distant Black middle-class to the masses. I also examine Walker's suggestion that a Black male "awakening" and sharing of responsibility must be a factor in the continued struggle if the community is going to progress.

Toni Cade Bambara's *The Salt Eaters* (1980) also focuses on spiritual awakenings, the power of Black female relationships, organizational decline, and the necessity of a continued struggle after the Civil Rights and Black Power movements have allegedly "ended." In Chapter Four, I read the protagonist (Velma Henry) as a freedom fighter who has vigilantly responded to the absence of insurgent action within her troubled Southern community with a spirit of rebellion. Through Bambara's representations of the fragmented self, gender politics, and the division of community-based coalitions, she provides a space to read Velma's attempted suicide as the impending destruction of the community. Velma's subsequent re-formation and own consciousness-raising spiritual experience renews her strength and determination to fight for her community, signaling the possibility of hope reclaimed.

Chapter Five expands the focus of Black American activism to incorporate global consciousness. Paule Marshall's *The Chosen Place, The Timeless People* (1969), set on a fictional Caribbean island, represents cross-cultural political action throughout the African Diaspora and the dangers of globalization from a notably Western subject position. Though chronologically, this novel predates the others, it enters into a long-standing conversation about Black Atlantic subjectivity and the shared African sociopolitical history in the New World. Within Chapter Five, I address the shift to feminist attempts at Third World coalition building during the Black revolutionary period. Here Marshall's text is applied to discuss the collaboration between Black American political history and Diasporic grassroots activism. I explore the role of the central Black female character Merle, her attitudes towards organized resistance within her island community, and how within the context of Black American political ideology the struggles of Black indigenous people globally must continue to be a relevant point of comparison.

The final chapter concludes the project by drawing together the importance of the novels as well as the aims and outcomes of the characters' lives and experiences. I reiterate the importance of revisiting fictional works written by Black women during the post-Civil Rights Movement and considering those writings blueprints for addressing challenges faced by members of the Black community. I argue that although the fiction of the Black Revolutionary period in 20th century American history was not the most "popular" form of disseminating information or raising consciousness, it was inarguably the most powerful. The authors surveyed in this project understand the work that can be done in the overlooked, forgotten places of society's consciousness. More specifically, the focus is on the radical fiction and "real revolution"[5] of Black women writers with the foresight to dig at the root of a social and racial dilemma, who in the end, anticipated the shifts taking place and advocated for community building through imagined possibilities.

Chapter Two

"Look Before You Leap"

Reading Black Nationalist Rhetoric and Toni Morrison's *Song of Solomon*

1964 will see the Negro revolt evolve and merge into the world-wide black revolution that has been taking place on this earth since 1945 . . . Revolutions are based upon bloodshed. Revolutions are never compromising. Revolutions are never based upon negotiations. Revolutions are never based upon any kind of tokenism whatsoever. Revolutions are never even based upon that which is begging a corrupt society or a corrupt system to accept us into it. Revolutions overturn systems. And there is no system on this earth which has proven itself more corrupt, more criminal, than this system that in 1964 still colonizes 22 million African-Americans, still enslaves 22 million Afro-Americans.

—Malcolm X (1964)

[W]e must recapture our heritage and our identity if we are ever to liberate ourselves from the bonds of White supremacy. We must launch a cultural revolution to unbrainwash an entire people.

We Afro-American people will launch a cultural revolution which will provide the means for restoring our identity that we might rejoin our brothers and sisters on the African continent, culturally, psychologically, economically and share with them the sweet fruits of freedom from oppression and independence of racist governments.

—Malcolm X (1965)

When discussing nationalism within the Black community,[1] one also has to understand the various forms, strands, and ideologies associated with this multi-layered concept. Due to the peculiar situation of Africans in America, the political standpoint of the community cannot be easily categorized, and/or understood as homogenous. For example, modes of what is termed "Black" Nationalism include (but are not limited to) Separatist, Integrationist, Anglo-Saxon, Anglo-African, Christian, Modern, Third World, Traditional, Radical, Post-colonial, Territorial, Cultural, Revolutionary, Afrocentric, and Post-nationalist.[2] Each mode represents the needs and/or demands of the community at various historical junctures. This variety does not make one "type" of nationalism more effective than another, but provides space for understanding the continuum of which the Black experience in America is a part. The first section of this chapter explores the contemporary history of revolutionary and cultural nationalism as understood in the context of fourth wave Black political revolution (1966–1976).[3]

There exists a multitude of articles, books, and case studies that address the role of Black Nationalism and/or Black Nationalist discourse in the forming of Black political identity. Recent scholarship has sought a reflective examination of historical precedents that inform "post-nationalist politics,"[4] while earlier works identify nationalism as the "Black man's" response to economic inequality and the "largely disadvantaged lower-class position," due to "racially based oppression" (Blair 4–5).

Historically, "New World" Black communities have responded to the need for Black national unity through liberation from a colonial regime. Because of the fractured connection to a common homeland (Africa) through the dispersal of Black peoples during the Trans-Atlantic Slave Trade, the quest for nationhood outside the African continent has been integral to the survival of New World black culture. Likewise, Black Nationalist organizations and movements in the Americas have maintained both cultural and political standpoints. Therefore, I read the advancement of cultural and revolutionary nationalist agendas as continuous processes integral to African American survival,[5] but through an understanding provided by Afro-Politico Womanism (APW) I analyze the flaws inherent in top-down leadership and a focus on individual gains in these agendas. Finally, I apply an *Afro-Politico Womanist* reading of Toni Morrison's *Song of Solomon* as a text that addresses the dangers of warring ideologies during a period of national social unrest.

NEW WORLD FOUNDATIONS

During the antebellum period, Black Nationalist ideology manifested in protest activity that ranged from Latin American and Caribbean slave insurrections to the subsequent founding of maroon colonies. These "colonies" existed as subversive responses to the mass colonization of African slaves and the attempts to completely destroy communal ties to African ancestral nations and culture. Of the maroon colonies, it is said,

"Regardless of the maroon society, community members established identities and spirituality apart from the social structure of the slaveholder's household. Maroon societies helped endure cultural survival" (National Park Service). Often, African fugitives sought shelter and aid from indigenous Indian or Native American tribes because they recognized similar cultural traits, practices, and family structures that made integration into their respective communities more acceptable.

Later, as an abolitionist strategy, Black church groups and social organizations mobilized in efforts to bring national attention to slavery's injustices. Though mainstream abolitionist rhetoric derided the immorality and inhumanity of American economic institutions, speeches given by Black leaders and fugitive slaves to anti-slavery advocates drew the connections to a flawed political system built upon prejudice and oppression (based on color, culture, and/or racial heritage). For example, in the speech "Our Heads Are in the Lion's Mouth" given by John S. Rock at the Annual Meeting of the Massachusetts Anti-Slavery Society in 1862, he condemns an American economy that benefits from the subjugation of "Negro" people, simply because they are Black. He writes,

> Had it not been for slavery, we should have had no war! Through 240 years of indescribable tortures, slavery has wrung out the blood, bones, and muscles of the Negro hundreds of millions of dollars, and helped much to make this nation rich . . . You are the only people, claiming to be civilized, who take away the rights of those whose color differs from your own . . . (in Wagstaff 10, 12–13)

In the Post-Reconstruction period, the violent social climate in the South and the desperate urgings of "Exodusters" convinced hundreds of Black families (and individual women) to go West, then North, then West again, in an effort to create and rebuild the healthy, thriving black communities that rarely existed outside of Jim Crow's grasp. On the surface, the list of Black nationalist efforts during the 20th century appears endless, including: individual Black settler communities working together to secure rights and justice under the restrictions of the American legal system in the West; the formation of national organizations (e.g. NAACP, NACW, Urban League) in an attempt to maintain a cohesive and subaltern Black national consciousness distinct, yet always a part of, the "American Experience;" the birth of the New Bourgeois Negro; the emergence of women's clubs and the "salvation" of young and uneducated black girls; Garveyism and the Back to Africa Movement; the formation of Black labor unions; Black support of socialism; Black Power, and so forth. The Black experience in

America is a composite of numerous social and political battles organized by black activists and intellectuals to achieve and maintain rights, progress, structure, pride, and stability within Black communities across the nation.

While the later move toward racial inclusiveness within political action was an important step in securing wider support for the Civil Rights Movement and the Black Power Movement,[6] historically, the black community's ability to organize and mobilize members for social change within a framework of separatism and segregation (albeit forced) has typically been its political strength. As the organizational structure of Black grass roots civil rights organizations of the 1960s transformed from ad-hoc to fully strategic bases of command after 1965, membership was "closed" to those groups with illegitimate interests and/or those who racially represented the opposition. For several leaders during the era, the importance of separation from outside groups was expressed through literature, speeches, and pamphlets used as tools for recruitment and education. In a 1966 essay titled, "Power and Racism," Stokely Carmichael (then still affiliated with SNCC) admonishes white liberals who desire acceptance within Black activist movements in the American South. He writes,

> White America will not face the problem of color, the reality of it. The well-intended say: 'We're all human, everybody is really decent, we must forget color.' But color cannot be 'forgotten' until its weight is recognized and dealt with. White America will not acknowledge that the ways in which this country sees itself are contradicted by being black—and always have been . . .
>
> Whites will not see that I, for example as a person oppressed because of my blackness, have common cause with other blacks who are oppressed because of blackness. This is not to say that there are no white people who see things as I do, but that it is black people I must speak to first. It must be the oppressed to whom SNCC addresses itself primarily, not to friends from the oppressing group (Carmichael 67–68).

Carmichael echoes earlier statements made by Black leaders like Malcolm X, who claimed that white America(ns) are unable to aid the Black community as long as whites are the only people in positions of power in America. The idea that a separate but equal Black nation was *needed* within the Black Revolutionary[7] movement directly contradicted earlier integrationist efforts by Civil Rights leaders. Subsequently, the idea that the American justice system could solve inequality by merging cultures and races within the classroom was also challenged within nationalist rhetoric. For many, the black community simply could not survive within the confines and/or limitations of a white American infrastructure.

The debate over separatism versus assimilation into the American mainstream (or accommodation versus revolution) reappears frequently as organizations with similar goals (Black liberation) contested the correct process for Black progress. For example, the rifts that existed between the leadership of the Nation of Islam (NOI), the Southern Christian Leadership Conference (SCLC), the Student Non-Violent Coordinating Committee (SNCC), The Black Panther Party for Self-Defense, and the US organization, were representative of a longer history of dissention among Black organizations.

While the continued support of a Black Nationalist agenda appeared to be a viable solution to American social ills in the 1960s, what the new, younger leaders of the Black Revolutionary movement did not fully anticipate was the enemy within. In 1969, Thomas Wagstaff notes,

> Other minority groups, preserving the sense of a common and respected heritage, have been able to draw closer together in the face of adversity and mount concerted countermeasures. The Negroes' frustration and anger at their continued exploitation and rejection has generally been directed not at their oppressors, but turned inward upon themselves (Wagstaff 2).

In an effort to distance the *new* revolutionary agenda from the conciliatory and "submissive" Civil Rights Movement, black activist-revolutionaries rejected and ignored the lessons that could be taught from past errors. What was not publicly televised or apparent during the Civil Rights Movement was the infighting, sexism, power plays, exclusion and self-destruction that moved the focus away from the specific goals of the "movement," to the inadequacies of leadership within cadre organizations. These same organizational issues challenged the success of the burgeoning Black Power movement, and also led to an unfortunate rift among its followers. In addition, Black Nationalism as a separatist ideology became further striated to include arguably distinctive "cultural" and "revolutionary" veins. Though culture and revolution as ways of situating the political position of the Black American have existed for decades, between 1965–1971 Black organizations, which comprised those veins, embarked on an ironic quest—fighting against each other to achieve the same goal.

Black Revolutionary Nationalism

The presence of the revolutionary in the New World Black community is constant. Without question, African Americans have existed within an antagonistic and toxic national environment from the year 1619 to the present. Given these circumstances the natural reaction of the oppressed has been to engage in what is deemed "revolutionary" activity in an effort to achieve total liberation, be it physical or psychological. For example, in the Caribbean and Americas during the eighteenth century, abhorrent conditions and treatment coupled with African cultural survivals provided an environment ripe for rebellion. In Jamaica alone "frequent slave revolts averaged 400 participants and laid the foundation for a powerful revolutionary tradition by the nineteenth century" (Confessions 15). In 1804, Toussaint L'Ouverture led a Haitian slave army that defeated Napoleon and the formidable French army, which made Haiti the first Black republic in the Western Hemisphere. While in 1831, Nat Turner's rebellion, one of the largest of its kind in America, surprised the residents of Southampton County, Virginia and reawakened fears among the white population. Both L'Ouverture and Turner based their insurgency on a divine mission to deliver Black people from the hands of Imperialism, which was a threat to the progress and survival of the chosen Black race. Likewise, voices like those of David Walker reasoned that the American "Negro" could only progress when his character and strength were taken seriously by White America.

From the era of the abolitionist through the rise of American communism in the early 20th century, organized groups and individual African American leaders have taken a revolutionary standpoint and spoken against America's racist social climate. This standpoint included the threat of arms, retaliation, and "justice" for (white) America in the name of the enslaved and oppressed African that toiled on her land. It is important to note that the recurrent threat of a Black uprising similar to slave rebellions and insurgency seen in years past was employed as a rhetorical wake-up call for a sleeping America. In terms of a *true* nationalist agenda, outspoken members of the Black community were *not* willing or prepared to overthrow the American government or exist as a separate nation-state, as is evident years later. Much of the writing from this period serves as a rallying cry for members of the Black community to act, rather than pontificate, and demand rather than ask for equality and political rights *within* America. For example, in 1833, orator and activist Maria Stewart admonishes her silent male counterparts,

> I am sensible that there are many highly intelligent men of color in these
> United States, in the force of whose arguments, doubtless, I should dis-
> cover my inferiority; but if they are blessed with wit and talent, friends
> and fortune, why have they not made themselves men of eminence, by

striving to take all the reproach that is cast upon the people of color, and in endeavoring to alleviate the woes of their brethren in bondage? (Stewart 1833)

Stewart later addresses the Colonization Society's attempts to create a separate nation for American Blacks in Africa,

But many powerful sons and daughters of Africa will shortly arise, who will put down vice and immorality among us, and . . . I am afraid they will spread horror and devastation around . . . They [whites] would drive us to a strange land. But before I go, the bayonet shall pierce me through. African rights and liberty is a subject that ought to fire the breast of every free man of color in the United States (Stewart 1833).[8]

Stewart's simultaneous acceptance and refusal of an inherent connection to her African heritage comes to signify the position of later Black revolutionary organizations. The Black revolutionary nationalist understands his/her position as an *American* oppressed person of color within the throes of white-inflicted injustice. Therefore, any change that results from a Black revolution is part of white America's responsibility to Blacks as American citizens, first. Stewart supports nation building as a strategy to ensure Black American survival and progress—in America.

At the turn of the Twentieth Century, Black organizations like the National Association for the Advancement of Colored People (NAACP) openly refuted attempts by emerging Black Nationalist groups who felt the only solution to the "Negro" problem was repatriation to Africa. For many, this would be a move that would ensure the progress and stability of the Black race. Like Stewart, NAACP leaders appreciated their heritage, but rejected the removal to an African homeland. They placed the onus on the American government and demanded equality, representation and freedom in America.

After mid-century, Black revolutionary nationalism made a slight shift in ideology from the earlier attempts to collapse all types of nationalism into one term. Black nationalists of the 1960s have been regarded as the more "militant" branch of Black nationalism compared to what was deemed "accomodationist" principles of the Civil Rights Movement.[9] According to scholar William Van Deburg, revolutionary nationalists tended to distance themselves from the "black militant" whose anger was a result of being "left out of the system" (Van Deburg 154). On the contrary, 1960's-era revolutionary nationalism was an anti-capitalist movement based in the teachings and scholarship of Malcolm X, Mao Tsetung, Karl Marx, Robert F. Williams,[10] and Frantz Fanon, among others. This form of nationalism is viewed as a standpoint based on activism, rhetoric, community organization, and self-defense. The prevailing belief among revolutionary nationalists is that the oppressed cannot be completely free until the entire "system" is overthrown (Van Deburg 153). Therefore, working within the system is not an option as long as there remains white power elite that oppresses and enslaves the lower classes. The revolutionary nationalist understands that the effects of colonization, subordination, and world domination affect all people of color who are subjected to economic degradation and social injustice.

The evolution of revolutionary nationalism during this period saw an increased emphasis on connecting with Third World peoples, and even poor and liberal whites. Though proponents of the revolutionary aims argued for a complete overthrow and restructuring of the American system, the theoretical basis for revolutionary ideology supported a coalition of victims—regardless of race—who sought to acquire their share of power. This acceptance of a shared class struggle that superseded racism and/or racial exclusion proved to be a contentious topic within many revolutionary organizations that viewed the "struggle" as specific to Black people. Groups like the Black Panther Party for Self-Defense "endorsed Malcolm's acceptance of alliance with whites once the black community was united and after white radicals had closed ranks in the struggle on the side of the oppressed" (Blair 93). The opposing argument was that there was no excuse for whites to be poor given the history of power and wealth they automatically benefit from due to the hue of their skin. Though the experiences of other minority groups were understood and supported, many "friends from the oppressing group," as they were described in the earlier Carmichael quote, were not welcome within the "colored" sphere.

Black Cultural Nationalism

Arguably, Black Cultural Nationalism serves as the vanguard model for all types of Black Nationalist ideology.[11] Incorporated in cultural nationalism is the belief that Black people cannot survive and/or progress within the limitations of an American superstructure, if they do not first know and accept their African identities and the visceral connection they have to their ancestral roots. The cultural nationalist understands the function and necessity of revolution, as the revolution is internal to the Black community with economic, social, and cultural advancement at the helm of a psychological racial transformation. This type of nationalism is based on the premise of cognitive liberation, or the belief that the ideological transformation of the Black community rests on an initial cognitive understanding of "Blackness," and/or an appreciation of ancestral origins, and self-pride. In *Fighting Words*, Patricia Hill Collins synthesizes prior definitions of Black cultural nationalism constructed by Molefi Asante, Franz Fanon, and Maulana Karenga—all scholars who theorized Black culture. She writes,

> Black cultural nationalism aims to reconstruct Black consciousness by replacing prevailing ideas about race with analyses that place the interests and needs of African people at the center of any discussion . . .
>
> Reconstructing Black history by locating the mythic past and the origins of the nation or the people is intended to build pride and commitment to the nation. These elements allegedly can be used to organize the Black consciousness of people of African descent [and] ideally enables members of the group to fight for the nation (Collins 160).

According to this concept, a group's cultural awareness is closely connected to political participation, the ability to uplift the masses, and nation building. Under this model, the masses must be informed, educated, and made aware of their political position within society for movement activity to occur. In short, Black political and social movements are only as powerful as the masses allow, through their own understanding of their needs. Black Cultural Nationalist ideology has manifested in various ways throughout African American history. From the first uprising on a slave ship to the mythical tale of the Igbo people who walked into the ocean off the coast of South Carolina and "flew" back home,[12] the cultural and ancestral connections to an African homeland remain evident.

During the 19th century many blacks were being recognized as intellectuals within the Black community. This was the first time in American history that there existed a sizable amount of recognized genius and a literate audience made up of their peers (Lively 207). Because of this "phenomenon," this was a crucial time for unity and self-empowerment. Many intellectuals looked towards the Bible as a source of redemption and interpreted passages as prophetic warnings of the changes to come. Out of this tradition, the biblical verse, "Envoys (princes) will come out of Egypt; Ethiopia will quickly stretch out her hands to God"[13] was the impetus for a movement of cultural awareness and change among Black intellectuals.

Many African Americans believed "Ethiopia" was a direct reference to Black people and racial challenges in American society. One of the themes of Black Nationalism was African repatriation, "a goal that dramatized opposition to the mainstream liberal and integrationist agenda" (Fitzgerald 294). Ethiopianism was a mobilization effort to establish a common Black identity. As with other ideologies, American civil religion was a main influence on Black Nationalism (Moses 28). In the late 19th to early 20th century the belief that the Ethiopia reference in the Bible was a direct representation of the oppressed American people gave hope to the thousands that felt there was no end to their psychological and physical bondage. Many felt that when Ethiopia did "stretch out her hands to God" the black community would rise up and take its rightful place in society. Black Nationalism and what was later termed "Ethiopianism," worked together to create a call for active change.

One of the most widely studied leaders in the cultural nationalist movement is Marcus Garvey.[14] As a leader, he was probably the most misunderstood and wrongly categorized Black cultural nationalist of the 20th century. Typically, scholars place Garvey, the Back to Africa Movement, and Garveyism, under the heading "Revolutionary Nationalism,"[15] but in actuality, his platform was more in line with a cultural nationalist agenda. In "Revolutionary Nationalism and the Afro-American," Harold Cruse remarks on Garvey's impact on the Black community. He writes,

> Garvey mobilized large sections of the discontented urban petit-bour-
> geois and working-class elements from the West Indies and the South
> into the greatest mass movement yet achieved in Negro history. The
> Garvey movement was revolutionary nationalism being expressed in
> the very heart of Western capitalism (Cruse 43).

Though Cruse contends that the "Garvey movement was *revolutionary nationalism*," what he terms "revolutionary" is not only a desire and drive to return to an African homeland, but several tenets closely associated with cultural nationalism. The most significant impact of the Garvey movement on the African Diaspora was the focus on economic development within Black communities, the construction of a Black nation apart from the limitations of America, an affirmation of pride in Africa, and cultural nationalist markers—uniforms, songs, flags, prose—which united movement participants. These same characteristics shape and define cultural nationalism after 1965 and become the platform upon which the US organization, led by Maulana Ron Karenga, built its agenda.

GENDERED READINGS

By tracing the Black intellectual traditions of Revolutionary and Cultural Nationalism, one can attest to the considerable impact both ideologies have had upon Black political movements. As well, in earlier years, both modes of nationalism played a significant role in restructuring Black consciousness as it connects with class and gender. Revolutionary nationalism, the will to fight for freedom and the use of self-defense tactics, can be traced to the vigilantism of Harriet Tubman, David Walker, Nat Turner, and many others. In recent years, the Black "revolution" is closely aligned with Robert Williams, Malcolm X, and the Black Panther Party for Self-Defense, among other individuals and organizations identified as anarchists and Black loyalists.

Cultural nationalism's quest was an initial awakening that would equal more than rumination on the status of the "Negro" in America and abroad, but a movement which understood internal change imagines external change. From Alexander Crummell, Maria Stewart, and Marcus Garvey through the Harlem Renaissance, Black Power and the formation of Black Studies programs, the cognitive liberation of Black people worldwide is the impetus for a closer examination of the possibilities for social advancement and economic parity. Unfortunately, in the 21st century, what historian Robin Kelley terms "Freedom Dreams," or the utopist imaginings of a liberated Black America—have yet to be realized.

Within Afro-Politico Womanism (APW) lies an inherent critique of Black Nationalism. This critique serves as an examination of how racial integration and organizational dissonance served as precursors to the structural demise of the Black community. While analysis of the various chasms within Black organizational structures throughout history could serve as a separate project unto itself, it is important to identify a few key examples as a means of justifying the need for a more harmonious method of imagining Black progress in the latter half of the 20th century.

Between 1900 and 1906, W.E.B. Du Bois and Booker T. Washington embarked on a notoriously contentious exploration of the "Negro" problem in America. What resulted was an ideological battle. Washington, a former slave and educator, believed that the most effective way to integrate the southern "Negro" into American society was by making "his" skills useful to whites and later to "his" community. Unlike Washington, Du Bois argued that the only way Blacks could possess power (and advance) in America was if they had the proper liberal arts education that would ensure integration into American national politics. The only hope for the Negro was to acquire the right to vote and enter into the political process that governs American life. In "Revolutionary Nationalism and the Afro-American" Harold Cruse notes, "There was much frustrated bickering and internal conflict within this new class over strategy and tactics. Finally the issues boiled down to that of *politics vs. economics*, and emerged in the Washington-Du Bois controversy" (Cruse 48)

In addition to Washington, Du Bois (as head of the NAACP and "leader" of the Black intellectual community) openly admonished Marcus Garvey's "Back to Africa" campaign. Du Bois believed that educated Black elite, or the "talented tenth percent" of the Black community, was destined to lead the Black race out of the valley of economic despair and social ostracism. In Garvey, he saw a zealot whose solution to the problems facing Blacks in America was to leave the country of their birth, for a mythical African homeland. For Garvey, the plan was not merely to send blacks back "home," but to send a select few with intellectual backgrounds in order that the preparation would not run the risk of corruption on the grounds of incompetence. Ironically, this aspect of the plan was similar to the "talented tenth" of Du Bois, a leader whom Garvey disliked in return. Not only did the two clash on the idea of repatriation, but also Garvey felt Dubois was not driven to incorporate the masses in his plan for upward mobility (Cruse 39–63).

Sixty years later, during the Black Power movement, Black revolutionary nationalists similarly despised cultural nationalists, this time for an allegedly absent political agenda and pacifist policies. The most notorious organizational feud is the fatal discord between members of the Black Panther Party for Self-Defense and the US organization.[16] The Black Panthers claimed to support a more radical agenda as they identified themselves as "revolutionaries" who put "theory into practice" when it came to overthrowing the racist American government. US believed, as did most cultural nationalists, that the *real* revolution begins in the mind. As stated earlier, the organization championed a psychological return to Africa, the adoption of African names and clothing, and an emphasis on building Black wealth.

Members of the Panthers accused cultural nationalists of being reactionary and bourgeois without a definite function or organizational agenda. In a 1969 speech, Fred Hampton, chairman of the Illinois Panther Party "instructed" his audience on the shortcomings of cultural nationalism, specifically as it was manifested as part of the US organization:

> Ron Karenga and US ain't never shot nothing but dope until they shot them brothers. Been an organization longer than the Black Panther

Party been an organization. And when the Black Panther Party stood up and said 'we ain't gone fight racism with racism,' US said 'naw, we can't do that because we know it's a race question, and if you make it a class question then the revolution might come sooner, and we and US ain't prepared for no revolution, because we thought, we think that political power grows from the sleeve of our dashiki.

And we in the war and we armed with rhetoric and rhetoric alone. And we found that when you armed with rhetoric and rhetoric alone then a lot of times you get yourself hurt . . . Cleaver said, 'we ain't going to fight racism with racism, we gone fight racism with solidarity.' Even though you think you need to fight capitalism with Black capitalism, we gon' fight capitalism with socialism (Hampton 1969, FICS Audio Archive).

In response to the negative press and vindictive statements made about his organizational practices, Maulana "Ron" Karenga contended that the forced separation of the two ideologies was useless. In *African American Nationalist Literature of the 1960s*, Sandra Hollin Flowers writes in response to the similarity between rhetorical stances,

> Karenga's assertion that it is erroneous to divorce cultural from revolutionary nationalism is not without support in nationalist history and theory. Nor, for that matter, was it without support in 1960s African American nationalist thinking, although it was more common for nationalists to array themselves in opposing camps (Flowers 35).

Of course, the divide between these forms of nationalisms followed other historic disagreements on the correct direction of the Black community that are not mentioned in full here. A few being non-violence vs. self-defense (or justified violence) as represented in the leadership of Martin Luther King, Jr. and Malcolm X, and the traditional Black Christian church vs. other Black religious organizations like the Nation of Islam or Black Christian Nationalism.

The *Afro-Politico Womanist* critique recognizes the fault of leadership within the organizations as well as the "erroneous" nature of their discord. The real issue at hand is not how one particular group imagines the quest for Black liberation, but who is allowed on the journey. With each of the examples listed above, the focus shifted from the fate and progress of the Black masses to the maintenance of particular leadership and/or an organizational base that neglects to consult the poor and working classes regarding their own fate. Afro-Politico Womanism asks, in short, can self-appointed leaders and externally defined organizations really represent the masses?

In a FOCUS magazine article on the impact female participation in the Civil Rights Movement had on movement politics, Britta Nelson quotes activist and organizer Ella Baker on the "issues" surrounding the Southern Christian Leadership Council's (SCLC) leader-focused agenda. She writes,

> In her view, the degree of adulation and dependence which the SCLC showed regarding King could not be healthy for the movement. [As Baker said], "Instead of trying to develop people around a leader, the thrust should be to develop leadership out of the group, and to spread the leadership roles so you're organizing people to be self-sufficient rather than to be dependent on . . . a charismatic leader . . . My theory is: strong people don't need strong leaders" (Nelson 4).

What Baker recognizes is the lack of progress and unhealthy atmosphere that exists when leaders and/or organizations are sovereign over the "masses" of people they are supposed to represent. What is evident in the historical and intellectual tradition of Black leadership in community activism is the emphasis on male-driven philosophies of struggle and a void as it relates to the "unity of interests . . . between middle and working classes" (Cruse 56). Class hierarchy remained a significant topic as the Black community moved from a pattern of non-violence to violence as rhetorical responses to the political climate.

For example, leaders within select revolutionary nationalist organizations frequently derided followers of Black cultural nationalism for being "pork-chop" nationalists, or bourgeois nationalists, and therefore detrimental to the fate of the Black proletariat. In *Black Nationalism in American Politics and Thought*, Dean Robinson defines "Bourgeois Nationalism" as "mild cultural pluralism with a politics that seeks expanded opportunities in American society" (Robinson 52). Later, Robinson quotes Robert Allen on Blacks who represented Bourgeois Nationalist goals in part by stating, "mostly middle-class blacks benefited from Black Nationalist proposals and that many of these welded 'black communities more firmly into the structure of American corporate capitalism'"(Robinson 89–90). Therefore, when revolutionary nationalists deemed it appropriate to identify Bourgeois nationalism as the political ideology from which the cultural nationalists theorized; they accused cultural nationalism of being a fraud. The argument was that cultural nationalists were removed from the working class and vested in the support of capitalism.

Though Huey Newton and Bobby Seale, (the founding members of the Black Panther Party for Self-Defense), were geographically from the "streets" of Oakland, California, the knowledge they acquired from Merritt College (Oakland City College) was more than "a bleak redoubt of urban education" (Blair 88). Both men were pivotal to the Black Power movement's emphasis on "theoretical underpinnings" and political participation. As leaders and students they had access to higher education and readily employed the political discourse of Frantz Fanon, Karl Marx, Mao Tsetung, Fidel Castro, Amil Cabral, etc. when theorizing on the current status of the Black community. Likewise, the organization attracted like-minded educated Black revolutionaries from middle-class families. What resulted was a movement based on rhetoric, theory, and the access to higher education. Though the emphasis on knowledge and political rhetoric was integral to the survival of the movement, the focus eventually shifted from the immediate needs of the poor and working classes. Whereas in the beginning the Breakfast for Children programs and Freedom Schools that fed and educated city children were pivotal, by the decline of the Bay Area based organization, members were steeped in "bureaucratic machinery,"[17] and the Black Panther Party had divided into "right wing" and "left wing" factions (Blair 88–90).

In "Poor Black Women's Study Papers: Letter to a North Vietnamese Sister from an Afro-American Woman—Sept. 1968," Patricia Robinson employs a Marxist understanding of bourgeois socialism.[18] In the *Communist Manifesto*, Marx and Engels define bourgeois socialism as existing for the benefit of the working class without disrupting the privileges and immediate needs of the bourgeois. Robinson critiques the complicit nature of the middle class black community and accuses capitalists of fostering an illusory atmosphere. She restates the logic of the power structure by stating, "Let the small middle class integrate, school them well in the role of puppets, and they will make excellent overseers— hence the Supreme Court decision of 1954 to integrate schools" (Robinson 190). Robinson identifies similar black bourgeois socialists as "the *Black radicals* who had analyzed the system as the enemy but had not the resources or followers to unite with the *poor Blacks*" (Robinson 190, emphasis mine). What Robinson argues for is a close examination of the divisions within the Black community that result from high theory and low expectations for the masses upon whom the leaders theorize.

The ideologies professed by Cultural and Revolutionary Nationalists denounce the overarching racism of the American government, and the psychological effects racial segregation has on marginalized masses. Both camps understand that the Black community will always be at a disadvantage if it does not rally around "Black Power." The problematic lay in the unfortunate varying approaches in achieving this power and what can be classified as immaturity in organizational leadership. In the end, the war of words eclipses the successes of Black activism, and the movements eventually dissipate.

CASE STUDY: *SONG OF SOLOMON*

The *Afro-Politico Womanist* agenda identifies the root of the struggle as lying within the poor and working class and Black female activism as continuously connected to the needs and desires of the root—or the community—with or without an externally defined movement. As this project examines the fictional representations of Black women's community activism and the merger between cultural and revolutionary nationalism as a framework for Black political progress, one needs to understand the full implications of Black women's visions for a whole society. As I have just outlined in this chapter, the political ideologies that comprise debates between leaders on the "correct" path for Black progress overshadow the plight of the Black community itself. Black women activists and novelists that fit under the Afro-politico Womanist model address the needs of the masses and embark on a practical journey, one that criticizes organizational discord and failed leadership.

An example of a literary text that incorporates Black political history as well as a critique of nationalist ideological battles is Toni Morrison's *Song of Solomon* (*SOS*). Though *SOS* was published in 1977, the characters exist in a continuum of Black political discourse from the opening sequence in 1931 to the novel's culmination in the mid 1960s. The strength of the novel is its ability to lay the groundwork for a discussion of continued activism and the future of Black political progress. Like the other fictional texts in this project, *SOS* serves as a cautionary tale, one that warns of the dangers of a shattered future if the Black community continues to privilege political rhetoric over the preservation of Black cultural traditions.

In the novel, the debate between cultural nationalism and revolutionary nationalism as pathways to Black liberation is represented in Morrison's characterization of Milkman Dead, Guitar Baines, and Milkman's aunt, Pilate Dead. Milkman and Guitar come of age in the post-migration North but learn they are not divorced from the cultural and political history that relegates poor, rural Black Southern communities to second-class status. The two young men are friends divided by economic privilege and social class—Milkman born into a comfortable Black middle-class family and Guitar, a member of the Black proletariat who reside on the "Southside." The third character, Pilate, is a symbol of the folk as she exhibits African centered traditional practices. As a maternal figure, her presence in the novel warns the present generation of a dangerous future if the focus does not shift from individualism to communal growth and responsibility.

As each male character struggles to understand his position within the larger socio-political landscape, Guitar chooses a militant revolutionary standpoint that envisions the revolution as a series of retaliatory acts—black against white—as the ultimate panacea for the injustices of white America. He joins the "Seven Days" society, a group of older Black men who decide that the only way frequent killings of innocent Black people by white racists will end is if innocent whites are killed also. Each member of the society is assigned a day of the week (Guitar's being Sunday) to carry out their mission for the love of Black people. Guitar explains,

> There is a society. It's made up of a few men who are willing to take some risks. They don't initiate anything; they don't even choose. They are as indifferent as rain. But when a Negro child, Negro woman, or Negro man is killed by whites and nothing is done about it by their law and their courts, this society selects a similar victim at random, and they execute him or her in a similar manner if they can . . . It got started in 1920, when that private from Georgia was killed after his balls were cut off and after that veteran was blinded when he came home from France in World War I. And it's been operating ever since. I am one of them now (Morrison 154–55).

Guitar's understanding of his duty to "save" Black people is based on the revolutionary rhetoric of the Black Power era. Milkman even accuses him of sounding "like that red-headed Negro named X," and he feels both fear and dread for his friend. Guitar is symbolic of the attitudes of young Black youth in the 1960s who were fed up with a capitalist, racist, and oppressive American government that did not respond to acts of domestic terrorism carried out in Black communities by white citizens. Enamored by the rhetoric of Black leaders like Malcolm X, they joined organizations or formed their own in an attempt to act in a way that would garner the attention and *fear* of White America. Whereas the violence inflicted on the Black body during the Civil Rights Movement continued to place the Black community under siege, the new agenda rejected a strategy of passivity and implemented a plan of action that would cause whites to take notice or possibly lose *their* lives.

Guitar's "revolutionary" speech and actions in *SOS* patterns popular Black male leaders outside the pages of the novel. For example, in video footage of a 1960s era Black Panther Party rally, Panther co-founder Bobby Seale addresses a recent "misprint" in a local newspaper. He points to the subtitle under a picture of fellow colleagues that called the organization reactionary and "anti-white. Seale refutes the accusation and explains, "We are not anti-white. We don't hate white people. We hate oppression . . . " (*Eyes on the Prize:* "Power!"). Similarly, Guitar explains of his participation in the Seven Days, "What I'm doing ain't about hating white people. It's about loving us. About loving you. My whole life is love" (Morrison 159). Guitar believes that the motive (love for Black people) justifies his actions and like many revolutionaries during the era concentrates on immediate outcomes while losing sight of the future. Later, he undergoes a philosophical, physical and spiritual transformation (no alcohol, no parties), and moves stealthily through the pages of the novel (stalking Milkman) appearing only as a reminder to Milkman to "watch [his] back," because "everyone wants the life of a black man."

Unlike Guitar who goes from being aware of his own depravity as a child to intensely aware of the institutional reasons for his marginalized status as an adult, Milkman's awakening is a much slower process. It is not until the last chapters in the novel that he is able to understand and appreciate his rich Black heritage. Milkman's cultural connections to an African history and ultimate appreciation of the Black Aesthetic mark him as symbolic of a cultural nationalist standpoint. As stated earlier, Cultural Nationalism is concerned with the connection to an African past and an appreciation of Black culture as a means of ultimate Black liberation. As a young man, Milkman is in constant battle with his present reality and lacks a primordial connection to his heritage. Though he spends much of the novel lost in immaturity and ignorance, Morrison hints early on at his greater significance and power in the novel.

When Milkman is a child, the women who visit Ruth (his mother) notice that he is "mysterious" and ask if he "came with a caul," like a package comes with instructions (10). This line of questioning is a reference to the belief in Black folk tradition that a baby born with the "caul" (amniotic sac) covering his/her body possesses "powers" and can often see into the spiritual realm and/or have visions. In *Granny Midwives and Black Women Writers*, Valerie Lee cites oral narratives (compiled by folklorist Carroll Rich) on the "types of power" a caul possesses. She writes,

"Those of Rich's informants who themselves were born with veils [another name for caul] testify of many types of power: the power to tell when someone will soon die; the power to know when others talk about you; and the power to cure thrush, a childhood disease that affects the tongue" (Lee 121).

In some communities it is believed that if such a birth occurs then the afterbirth must be immediately buried under a tree to prevent the pre-monitions and "spirits" from haunting the child. In *SOS*, Ruth never answers the question, but asks if her guests "believe that," as if searching for her own answers through their possible acceptance of the "old" tra-ditions. Morrison shifts the focus to Milkman's uneasy disposition dur-ing the conversation and the reader is left with the possibility that the boy does possess an ethno-spiritual power that may soon be revealed.

There are other significant characteristics associated with Milk-man's birth that closely connect him to an African cultural tradition. The day before he is born, Robert Smith, a member of the Seven Days, decides he cannot handle his "love" for the people and leaps off Mercy Hospital's roof. This act foreshadows Milkman's own understanding of the power of flight as well as the myth of the "Flying Africans,"[19] of which his great-grandfather was associated. It is also revealed that Milk-man notices one of his legs is shorter than the other when he is fourteen years of age (Morrison 62). This physical characteristic is symbolic of his connection to Legba, an African deity who is labeled the "god of fate." Legba functions as a guide (and trickster) who leads others on a fateful journey. He, like Milkman, is often depicted as walking with a limp and has one leg shorter than the other. Naturally, it is not until Milkman begins to recognize his own path that his legs become even.

In another childhood scene as Milkman rides in the car with his family during a Sunday outing he is described as having to sit on his knees facing the back window because he is too small to see over the dashboard of the car. Milkman is forced to watch the people and trees go by without knowing what lies ahead. Later, Morrison writes, "It was becoming a habit—this con-centration on things behind him. Almost as though there were no future to be had" (35). What Milkman comes to understand is that his obsession with his unknown past speaks to a void that prohibits him from knowing himself. The above examples exhibit Milkman's spiritual connection to an African past that he *must* find and accept in order to survive. In "Reclaiming the Lost African Heritage," John Henrik Clarke speaks to this acceptance when he writes, " . . . Many writers and scholars, both black and white, have pointed to a rich and ancient African heritage, which, in my opinion, must be reclaimed if American Negroes in general and Negro writers in particular are ever to be reconciled with their roots" (Clarke 11).

Later, during his Homeric quest to find the key to his family's history, Milkman serves as his own guide through the physical terrain of Pennsylvania and Virginia. He begins to thirst for the unknown as he sheds the cocoon of materialism and becomes intoxicated with the songs, words, sayings, folklore, and simplicity of the Black community in the Blue Ridge Mountains. Morrison writes,

> He was curious about these people. He didn't feel close to them, but he did feel connected, as though there was some cord or pulse or information they shared . . . . But there was something he felt now—here in Shalimar, and earlier in Danville—that reminded him of how he used to feel in Pilate's house. Sitting in Susan Byrd's living room, lying with Sweet, eating with those men at Vernell's table, he didn't have to get over, to turn on, or up, or even out (Morrison 293).

The people he encounters are part of a canvas that reflects the essence of Black culture. In "Black Cultural Nationalism," Ron Karenga asserts, "All we do and create, then, is based on tradition and reason, that is to say, on foundation and movement. For we begin to build on traditional foundation, but it is out of movement, that is experience, that we complete our creation" (Karenga 33). Milkman's "creation" is an inner quest for his African-ness. Each step draws him closer to the story of the flying African Solomon (or Shalimar) and his scattered descendants, symbolic of an African Diaspora that pulsates throughout the world. As Milkman concludes his quest and is able to piece together "the puzzle" of his family history, he returns to Michigan to gather Pilate and bring her to the "home" she searched for her entire life, but could never find.

Symbolically, Pilate exists as a merger between Milkman's cultural nationalist characteristics and Guitar's revolutionary militancy. She is a folk character with ancient features and habits, yet, like Guitar, she will kill without warning for those she loves. For example, in a scene where her daughter Reba is attacked by a lover, Pilate jabs a knife in his chest and warns him, "Women are foolish, you know, and mammas are the most foolish of all" (92). Pilate lives as a rebel, outside of the institutionalized norms of the community. By having no navel and being named after "the man who killed Jesus," she is defined by opposition to what is deemed "correct." Her revolutionary standpoint includes not submitting to the orders or hierarchies of a capitalist society. She does not pay bills, associate with financial institutions, and runs an unlicensed "winehouse," during prohibition and beyond. She believes in an ancient spirituality that in essence "kills" the Christianity that so many in her community rely upon.

Simultaneously, as a symbol of cultural nationalism, "Pilate's various connections to Africa are unmistakable" (Lee 112). She possesses the knowledge of "roots," or herbal medicine ("greenish-gray grassy-looking stuff"), communicates in song, and exists as part of an African cultural continuum. In a scene when Milkman and Guitar are arrested after stealing a bag of human bones from Pilate's house, she is the only person able to aid in their release from jail. Pilate uses her "power" to delude the white policeman and in the process of telling a contrived story about her dead husband, she morphs into an alternate character, becoming simple and ignorant while simultaneously altering her height. Alma Billingslea-Brown makes this observation in *Crossing Borders Through Folklore*. She notes, "Morrison manipulates, in this passage, the reader's perceptual and sensuous experience in such a way as to demand active participation. To 'fill in the gap,' the reader must adhere to belief or willingly suspend disbelief in Pilate's magic" (Billingslea-Brown 49). Pilate's "magic," knowledge of an ancient world, and preservation of surviving rituals connects her to an African Diasporic consciousness. In "Black Arts: Notebook," John O'Neal writes, "The concept of home and roots in America is the problem. People can only bring a nation out of mutual commitment to their common good. Here, we have simply been victims. Our concept must be a world concept, and we must see our roots as African. We are an African people" (O'Neal 47). At the end of the novel, when Pilate returns to Virginia with Milkman, it is understood that she is returning not only to her parents' roots, but to the land that is forever connected to an African history in America—a geographic space her African grandfather literally "flew away" from (and tried to take her father with him).

The novel's finale is integral to an understanding of how *SOS* speaks to both the hopeful possibilities for the community and the threat of destruction during the Black revolutionary era. Morrison places Guitar and Milkman at a crossroads that represents life or death for the Black community. Guitar tracks Milkman throughout the wilderness and stalks his every move, as he does the white victims of his "love" for the Black race. In an earlier scene, Guitar speaks of Milkman's father, Macon Dead. He says, " . . . I don't have to tell you that your father is a very strange Negro. He'll reap the benefits of what we sow, and there's nothing we can do about that. He behaves like a white man, thinks like a white man" (Morrison 223). Where Guitar was aware of the Dead family legacy, but able to divorce Milkman from his heritage before, by the end of the novel he truly views Milkman as the product of Macon's "white" lineage. In Guitar's eyes, Milkman benefits directly from his father's economic privilege and is also a threat to the Black community. Therefore, the "son's day" (Sunday) has come. Milkman's attitude and actions pre-Virginia are representative of a middle-class mobility that places the Black proletariat in the rear-view mirror of Black progress. Guitar views Milkman's middle-class bourgeois existence as the real threat to the Black masses he claims to represent and protect, therefore it is his responsibility to "even the ratio."

However, Guitar does not recognize that while he has been chasing his friend/foe, Milkman has a concurrent transformation and has acknowledged his spiritual and cultural connection to his African and American heritage. He revels in the laughter of children who play a ring game based on his ancestral history, learns the power of Black love through his protective feelings toward Pilate and his relationships with Hagar and Sweet; he baptizes himself in mountain ridge water while singing words in an African tongue, and claims the aerial powers of his African grandfather. Milkman's euphoria is not only a product of self-identification, but also his reclamation of cultural heritage and pride.

When Milkman and Pilate arrive in Virginia and find an appropriate place to bury her father's bones, Morrison writes that as Pilate opened the bag, "a deep sigh escaped" and "a spicy sugared ginger smell, enveloped them" (335). The sigh appears to signal multiple expressions of relief: relief that the remains have finally returned home, relief that the trinity of Diasporic consciousness (Macon Sr., Pilate, and Milkman) is complete, and the relief of a spiritual release. After Guitar squats in the shadows and shoots Pilate, she releases another sigh—one of love (336). She laments, 'I wish I'd a knowed more people. I would of loved 'em all. If I'd a knowed more, I would a loved more' (336).

Pilate is killed because she stands in the crossfire of Guitar's militant revolutionary nationalist philosophy and Milkman's cultural nationalist appreciation of an African past. Pilate is symbolic of the "masses," a community caught between the ideological shifts within Black leadership during a period of social unrest and political instability. The community, like Pilate, ultimately becomes a silent victim of a war of words that neglects the needs and the lives of the people. Throughout the novel, Milkman and Guitar engage in a battle over who loves the community more, in the same ways that revolutionaries and culturalists are at odds over definitions and concepts. In an interview with *The Movement*, for example, Huey Newton speaks of his rejection of cultural nationalism. He explains,

> Cultural nationalism, or pork-chop nationalism, as I sometimes call it, is basically a problem of having the wrong political perspective. It seems to be a reaction instead of responding to political oppression. The cultural nationalists are concerned with returning to the old African culture and

thereby regaining their identity and freedom. In other words, they feel
that the African culture will automatically bring political freedom . . .
We believe that culture alone will not liberate us. We're going to need
some stronger stuff (as qtd. in Foner 50).

Newton reads the contributions of the cultural nationalists as counter-revo-
lutionary in all imaginings of the term. For Newton, the leader of one of
the most influential revolutionary nationalist organizations during the Black
Power movement, a return to African culture is "old" and unnecessary.
Cultural affirmation and pride were not a means to an end, only a stop on
the journey. In the same timeframe of Newton's comments, *Black Fire: An
Anthology of Afro-American Writing* was published. The immense collec-
tion of writings combines Black theory and Black Art as a means of connecting aesthetic and prophetic ruminations on the revolution. The editors, Leroi
Jones (Amiri Baraka) and Larry Neal, both proclaimed cultural nationalism
and the power of the Black Aesthetic to be liberating forces in Black American consciousness. Not surprisingly, some of the writings speak to an ideological rift between nationalist concepts. A portion of Edward Spriggs,' poem
"For the TRUTH (because it is necessary)" alludes to this rift:

> What kind of man are you/black revolutionary, so-called?/what kind
> of man are you trying to be/ultra-hip-revolutionary-nationalist/quasi-
> strategist-ego-centric-phony/intellectual romantic black prima donna
> child/—screaming, 'revolution means change . . . '/never finishing the
> sentence/or the thought/talking about 'para-military'/strategy and tech-
> niques/publicizing a so-called underground program/wearing your mili-
> tary garb/as if you never heard of camouflage/so in love with intrigue/you
> have no thoughts/about the post-revolution life/that the total destruction/
> you talk about assumes . . . (Spriggs 339–40).

The persona in the poem harangues the pseudo-revolutionary for his lack of
vision for a post-revolutionary society and for his destructive rhetoric. The
fact that the "revolutionary" has no plans for the future, but instead talks
of "'para-military' strategy" questions the survival of the Black community
after the revolution comes. Once everything is destroyed, who will be left?
Who is ensuring the future?

Similarly, in *SOS*, Pilate's death is a warning to young Black leadership that claims to act on behalf of "the people," but uses its power to
proselytize and destroy. Though Guitar works as an agent for the community, his murder of Pilate is a direct repudiation of the history she represents, as is his previous hunting of Milkman. He has "jeweled hatred" for

her—not realizing that the power is in her knowing *how* to save Black lives (210). Likewise, when Milkman realizes Pilate is dead, he leaps out into the darkness toward Guitar, unconcerned with the outcome. Morrison writes, "As fleet and bright as a lodestar he wheeled toward Guitar and it did not matter which one of them would give up his ghost in the killing arms of his brother" (337).

Milkman's flight toward Guitar is symbolic of a continuation of ideological warfare. The darkness that envelops both men as Pilate's crumpled body lies on the earth, symbolizes the unknown future and possible death of the community. Instead of preventing Pilate's death or even remaining with her after she dies, Milkman turns his hurt, sadness, and frustration back on Guitar. Similarly, young Black leaders of the Black revolution became obsessed with their distrust of and disenchantment with one another, abandoning the dying community and focusing their energy on intra-racial destruction. *SOS* shows that it *does* matter, who "gives up his ghost." In the end, neither Milkman nor Guitar learn the most important lesson of the quest: 'you just can't fly on off and leave a body,' or a community behind.

Chapter Three

"Tomorrow the People Would Come"

The Crisis of the Black Middle Class in Alice Walker's *Meridian*

We who have watched our young grow too old too soon; we who have watched our children come home angry and frustrated and see them grow more bitter and more disillusioned with the passing of each day; and we who have seen the sick, trapped looks on the faces of our children when they come to fully realize what it means to be Black in America.

—Assata Shakur
Activist

. . . .

You can pray until you faint. But if you don't get up and try to do something, God is not going to put it in your lap. And there's no need of running and no need of saying 'honey I am not going to get in the mess,' because if you were born in America with a black face you were born in the mess.

—Fannie Lou Hamer
Mississippi Freedom Democratic Party

In her seminal text , *In Search of Our Mother's Gardens*, Alice Walker comments on the alleged "death" of the Civil Rights Movement in 1967. She writes, "the Civil Rights Movement is only dead to the white media." She later explains that the Movement suffered from quasi-victories and landmark moments and through it all the focus remained on the sensationalized and televised aspects of the Movement, its marches, singing, and non-violent resistance. Walker solemnly notes, "No real effects of the Movement are ever noted such as human attitudes, changes in personal lives, etc." (120–1). Walker's sentiments about how the "real" revolution was taking place outside of public spectacle speak to the uncategorized "movement" which included individual lives, emotion, feelings, love, education, and experiences. Like Nina Simone's inquiry in the bluesy "Do I Move You?" (1966) Walker's vision of the progressive changes within the Black community demanded a spiritual inner-journey that moved from the "head down to the liver." She imagined a complete soul transformation.

Over the years, Walker has stated that she considers her work a part of her own commitment to the salvation of the Black community and female participation in the community. As a volunteer during the "Freedom Summer" voter registration drive in the Civil Rights south, her lived experience allowed her to create fiction, poetry, and critical writing from a place of personal experience and observation. Although often overlooked when analyzing social movements, lived experience is a necessary component of activist scholarship. In "The Social Construction of Black Feminist Thought," Patricia Hill Collins states,

> For ordinary African-American women, those individuals who have lived through the experiences about which they claim to be experts are more believable and credible than those who have merely read or thought about such experiences. Thus, concrete experience as a criterion for credibility frequently is invoked by Black women when making knowledge claims (Collins 190).

Collins further notes that women of color employ experiential knowledge when defining a theoretical standpoint. Specifically, if one considers Walker and the "imagined community" of Civil Rights workers and poor, rural Blacks in her novel, *Meridian*, it can be argued that Walker's practical experiences and knowledge about the rural "folk" place her at a theoretical advantage over others who attempt to construct similar narratives without the depth of experience.

Likewise, it is important to acknowledge the connections between Black female activism and literary production reaching as far back as the 18th century. For example, the poet Phillis Wheatley's own position as an African slave is directly tied to her often misunderstood and/or veiled references to liberation and oppression within her creative work. Similarly, women writer/activists of the 20th /21st century use their creative and political freedoms to effect change. The often used phrase "using words as a weapon," describes one of the many ways black women entered into the struggle for equality and justice, from the journalistic roots of Ida B. Wells that served as the foundation for an anti-lynching campaign, to Alice Walker's own student activism and SNCC membership that is the premise for her first two novels—"the artist is the voice of the people and she is the people" (Walker 138).

Alice Walker's *Meridian* places Black women at the center of the Marxist notion that social uprising is inevitable once the oppressed are aware of unjust material conditions. Moreover, the novel resists the notion that Black male Nationalists are the only individuals qualified to participate in Black America's political struggle, within and beyond the 1960s. The novel's main character, Meridian Hill, exists as a freedom fighter, understanding that continued struggle and support are required for the monolithic Black community to repair fractured relationships, internally. As a Black woman, her individual decision to pursue justice and equality despite ideological challenges to her position becomes symbolic of the endurance of grass roots workers operating in forgotten poor communities. Against the urgings of her family and friends Meridian continually champions the plight of her southern communities in a self-sacrificing manner, and is moved to action by her own spiritual, political, emotional, personal, cultural, and revolutionary experiences. In "Women in the Civil Rights Movement: Reform or Revolution?" Rhoda Lois Blumberg discusses female self-sacrifice in revolutionary movements, an analysis that can also be applied to *Meridian*. She writes:

> Self-sacrifice is a characteristic of women's gender roles that has often been considered normal. Reliance on intrinsic emotional and spiritual rewards, rather than gains in finances or status, is not unusual. In fact, women have often found it easier to struggle for other groups or causes than for themselves as women. In this case [the Black movements of the 1960s] black women, young and old responded with enthusiasm and bravery to the calls for sacrifice (Blumberg 82).

In Meridian Hill, Alice Walker creates a character who willingly gives her life to the cause of empowering the masses. Like Blumberg's description above, Meridian's purpose rests in her ability to struggle for those who lack the means, support, and/or education to fight on their own behalf. During this period in Black political history two (of many) opposite realities were present. 1.) Many beneficiaries of the economic struggle (i.e.; Black Middle Class) assimilated into corporate and academic positions or retreated to private spaces that did not include the Black masses who were the foundation of their progress. 2.) Several movement activists used the victories won in the 1960s as trajectories for continued work within poor and working class communities.

In this chapter, I classify Meridian's refusal to surrender at the "end" of the Civil Rights and Black Power movements as an APW standpoint which connects theory and rhetoric to practice in ways that her male counterpart in the novel (Truman Held) cannot accept. Through this lens, the characters Meridian Hill and Truman Held become symbolic of the crossroads in Black activism and leadership after the externally-defined end of the Civil Rights Movement. I read Truman Held as symbolic of an amnesiac Black middle class that emerges in the space following heightened levels of Black political activism in the 1960s. In her 1973 essay "Choosing to Stay Home" Walker contends, "The new Black middle class has forgotten the point of the fight and is complacent in its search for wealth and material objects" (Walker 168–9). Truman's frequent departures and returns (in and out of Meridian's life) represent the fluctuation of middle-class political ideology, as he moves between liberal activism, moderate intellectualism, and conservative indifference.

Conversely, Meridian represents a contingent of female movement activists who understand that to effectively support and ensure the perpetual progress of the Black community they must forever remain connected to and working for underrepresented masses. While Truman phases in and out of the struggle, Meridian remains in the south, working to ensure that small civil rights victories continue. Her activist standpoint involves a conscious rejection of established institutionalized norms that function as obstacles to community awareness and political progress. Though she questions whether the "revolution like everything else was reduced to a fad," her belief in the promise of the Black community does not allow her to abandon those she loves.

"Running off as soon as black became beautiful . . . "

–Lynne Held

As one of the only fully developed Black male characters in the novel, Truman Held's spiritual distance from the Movement and limited understanding of the individuals who make up the body speaks to the failure of male leadership to truly acknowledge the grand narrative of Black experience. For Truman, Black activism is episodic, de-contextualized, and generally devoid of a historical or intellectual tradition. His reactionary responses to racial injustice supply the basis for his inability to completely connect with the masses of poor and lower-class Blacks in the south. Like many liberal participants in the "movement" he recognizes the shame of segregation and discrimination, but is unable/unwilling to consider the masses outside of their immediate needs as he understands them (enfranchisement, desegregation, representation, etc.).

As the narrative progresses, the reader finds through various flashbacks and dream sequences that Truman has returned to Meridian (the locale, the woman) several times in the years following the Civil Rights Movement and his work as a community organizer in the South. Though the organization Truman works with in his younger years is never mentioned and the "movement" he is involved with is vaguely identified as "Civil Rights," the informed reader understands the connections Walker makes between the Student Non-Violent Coordinating Committee (SNCC) and Truman's experiences as a student leader in the Movement. These historical truths that blur the line between fact and fiction in the novel exist as a nebulous hyper-reality that combine Truman's own political awakening during the 1960s with that of America.

From an outsider's perspective, Truman's actions in the novel can be read as mile markers for Black political progress. According to hegemonic versions of American history, Black American experience occurs only within a few key titular moments: "Slavery," "Reconstruction," "The Harlem Renaissance," "The Civil Rights Movement," "Black Power," etc. These categories are reduced to moments in time, each denoting a specific era of change. The problematic is the same when social scientists identify Black social uprising (rioting, protests) as sporadic, not existing on a continuum but as unrelated spontaneous reactions to a particular moment of injustice. In the novel, Truman's character represents these schematic viewpoints. He embodies the attitudes of the Black middle class as he rapidly shifts from grass roots activist to distant intellectual, while also adopting superficial aspects of revolutionary nationalism and a modified form of cultural nationalism, before rejecting it all for a bohemian lifestyle.

Walker is savvy in presenting Truman as a troubled Everyman, one who morphs at the turn of the next page. Though her critique of the Black middle class is evident throughout the novel, it is especially biting when Truman's instability is closely examined. His peripatetic presence is always in opposition to Meridian's steadfast determination to exist for "the people," and sacrifice her own health. For example, after he abandons "the struggle" for his artistic endeavors he remains disconnected from Black poor and working class communities. In an exchange between Meridian and Truman in the 1970s, Meridian contemplates whether she should actually kill for the revolution, a question that has haunted her since she was first asked years ago by a group of militant young black women. She contemplates teaching, rather than killing, as a viable impetus for the revolution. Truman replies:

> Do you realize that no one is thinking about these things anymore? Revolution was the theme of the sixties: Medgar, Malcolm, Martin, George, Angela Davis, the Panthers, people blowing up buildings and each other. But all that is gone now . . .

After Meridian asks if he thinks revolution was "reduced to a fad," he replies:

> Of course . . . the leaders were killed, the restless young were bought off with anti-poverty jobs, and the clothing styles of the poor were copied by Seventh Avenue. And you know how many middle-class white girls from Brooklyn started wearing kinky hair (206).

Though Truman's statements are couched in fact—the reality around him—Meridian does not/cannot accept them as the final truth. In the 1970s Truman, and the rest of Black America, considers survival the only option left. People are living, working, and existing to survive, not for each other; a reality that Truman wants Meridian to accept. For Truman at this point in his consciousness the revolution and Black organizational leadership are dead, even though ten years earlier he ascribed to a different "truth."

In 1960, when Meridian and Truman initially meet, he is one of the leaders of a voter registration effort in Georgia. The house the group occupied previously has been bombed, and the news of the act causes Meridian to volunteer for duty. At this stage in his life Truman is a college student and one of the young, fearless members of the Black middle class whose *education* has taught them that the conditions in the South are intolerable. He thrusts himself into the movement and views his deeds as a service to the poor community, not unlike the white students who later arrive during what is realistically portrayed in the novel as "Freedom Summer." Significantly, the reader views Truman's physical activism through Meridian's eyes. In the section titled, "Battle Fatigue," Meridian recalls,

> Truman Held was the first of the Civil Rights workers—for that's what they were called—who began to mean something to her, though it was months after their initial meeting that she knew. It was not until one night when first he, then she, was arrested for demonstrating outside the local jail, and then beaten (Walker 80).

After this incident, Meridian finds Truman "limping" and his eyes "swollen and red, his body trembling." He is so weary he does not even recognize Meridian. He is quickly carried off in another police car before she can go to him. After that moment, Truman disappears from the "movement," while Meridian's continues to bear physical attacks upon her body during other marches and protests.[1]

After Meridian enrolls in Saxon College[2] (across the street from his own university, R. Baron College), Truman represents himself as a Black intellectual, reminiscent of a Duboisian era that charged the "New Negro" with leading the poor, black masses into a new century. He is urbane, well-traveled, speaks French, and dresses in impressive attire. In the section aptly titled, "The Conquering Prince," Truman displays his new "character" as he and Meridian are en route to a social gathering. As a testament to his cultured intellectualism he arrives in "a flowing Ethiopian robe of extravagantly embroidered white," and responds to Meridian's complements with "*Et toi aussi. Tu es très magnifique!*"(99). He later tells her in bits of English and French that he is glad she decided to attend Saxon because, "[She was] going to waste away out there in the sticks" (100). As their relationship progresses, Truman's overall attitude is that he is intellectually and culturally superior to Meridian's rural ignorance. He accuses her of being young and intolerant, and in a later exchange tells her that he prefers the company of two visiting white exchange students because "they read the *New York Times*" (152). He also confesses to himself, "although [. . .] the rich were a cancer on the world, he would not mind being rich himself" (205).

After reading *The Souls of Black Folk* by W.E.B. Dubois, he approaches Meridian with a new understanding of himself reflected in the passage below:

> He was startled by the coolness with which she received his assertion that what he had decided, after reading "*le maître,*" was that if he dated white girls it must be, essentially, a matter of sex. She laughed when she saw he expected her to be pleased and reassured, a bitter laugh that sent him away again, his chin thrust forward against her misunderstanding (107–8).

Truman misunderstands what he believes is Meridian's own "misunderstanding." In fact, it is Meridian who balks at his immaturity and considers a discussion of the text "too deep for Truman." Their readings differ, as their preferences differ—his being the current popular trend (white women) and hers, the intellectual relevance of the text. What Truman fails to realize is that when defined within the Black community, the "Negro problem" (discussed in the first few pages of Dubois' text), is not really a problem at all. But when Black people are placed in opposition to the white majority, the dehumanizing effects of bondage recycled for hundreds of years leads to psychological destruction. Adopting a Cleaverian[3] rationale for his own feelings of inferiority and powerlessness not only detracts from the depth of DuBois' observations, but also exposes Truman's hypocrisy. Meridian does not allow Truman to rationalize his personal identity crisis by (mis)reading

Dubois, neither can he expect her to understand his rejection of black womanhood and *not* feel "ashamed, as if she were less" (108).

As Truman transitions from activist to pseudo-intellectual he exemplifies the philosophies of bourgeois socialism, a shift repeated by many Black leaders during the post-Civil Rights era. Truman is not willing to compromise his status as a member of the Black middle class even as he acknowledges the injustices around him. He has the privilege of working in the rural South for "the summer" but returns "up Atlanta" when the school year begins. He has access to higher education and rides in his father's "new red car," and after graduation chooses to live as an artist in New York. His actions are symbolic of his liberal views and the liberalism of the era. He is a sympathizer to the plight of the oppressed, but like his white counterparts, he does not *have* to continue to fight "their" battles after the politics of race and justice are deemed passé.

In "Women as Culture Carriers in the Civil Rights Movement: Fannie Lou Hamer," Bernice Johnson Reagon documents Fannie Lou Hamer's contribution to the fight for equality in Mississippi. Reagon recalls Hamer's opinion on the divide between middle and lower class Blacks, specifically college-educated women (and men) who "had difficulty embracing her as their sister" (Reagon 213). Hamer speaks in 1971:

> A few years ago throughout the country the middle class Black women—I used to say not really Black women, but the middle class colored women, didn't respect the kind of work that I was doing. But you see now baby, whether you have a ph.d., dd, or no d, we're in this bag together. And whether you are from Morehouse[4] or Nohouse, we're still in this bag together" (Reagon 214).

Hamer's experiences with intraracial discrimination on the basis of class speak to inherent problems within a movement where many individuals viewed discrimination as being an economic, rather than a social ill. While speeches by notables like King, X, Carmichael, and Brown lambasted the inhumanity of discrimination and oppression—the bottom line was political equality and the protection of civil rights under the law which would lead to economic advancement. Ultimately, the goals and eventual outcomes addressed wealth and achievement gaps that continued to be supported by philosophies of inferiority and racism. In short, once discrimination in the areas that ensured prosperity (education, the labor market, and politics) was *legally* eradicated, more Black Americans would be able to sit at the table. Black economic power was the ultimate goal.

During this stage in his maturation Truman views southern Blacks as backwards or infantile in their ignorance. Instead, he identifies with a Northern cosmopolitanism that borders on elitism as he develops a completely bourgeois sensibility. For him at this point, the "movement" is attractive because it consists of charismatic and educated leaders—not the proletariat who reside in "the sticks." The problematic with this middle class standpoint is expressed by Dr. Martin Luther King, Jr. in his seminal text, *Where are We Now: Chaos or Community?* (1968). King reflects on a divided Black America when he asks:

> How many Negroes who have achieved educational and economic security have forgotten that they are where they are because of the support of faceless, unlettered and unheralded Negroes who did ordinary jobs in an extraordinary way? How many successful Negroes have forgotten that uneducated and poverty-stricken mothers and fathers often worked until their eyebrows were scorched and their hand bruised so that their children could get an education? For any middle-class Negro to forget the masses is an act not only of neglect but of shameful ingratitude (King 132).

At other points in the novel *Meridian*, Truman appears to reject his classist stance and instead reinvents himself as an advocate of Black Power (an ideology that consists of several layers). When Stokely Carmichael codified Black southern frustrations in 1966 and made "Black Power" a mantra for the youth movement, his main emphasis was on the lack of political power Black Americans have in the electoral process. Truman, on the other hand, misses this important element of Black Power philosophy and shirks the politics of the movement. His interests lay in affirming Black manhood (at the cost of *all* women), misguided Afrocentricity, and celebrating "militant" rhetoric.

Truman embraces what he identifies as "Black Power" and exerts his masculinity in ways that appear to meld Black revolutionary and cultural nationalism into one philosophy. He tells Meridian to walk with her head up "proud and free" and proclaims "Black is beautiful." In the same vein he pleads with her to "have [his] black babies," obviously forgetting that he fled earlier when he found out she was previously married and gave up her first child before coming to college (Walker 119–120). Truman couches his physical desires for Meridian in the Black Nationalist philosophy that the antidote for Black "genocide" is the mass reproduction of Black babies, (mini soldiers for the "revolution") with women's gynecological and psychological wellness notwithstanding. In *Fighting Words*, Patricia Hill

Collins notes, "Black nationalist projects of the 1960s often opposed contraceptive and reproductive services for African-American women, viewing such services as genocide" (Collins 170). Likewise, Patricia Robinson challenges the concept of birthing Black soldiers in *Poor Black Women* (1968), when she includes a reply from a group of "black sisters" to "the Brothers" who claim "when [they] produce children, [they] are aiding the REVOLUTION in the form of NATION building" (Robinson 1). Robinson's "women" blame Black male desertion after childbirth for an increased use of birth control among poor Black women and later cite birth control as "the first step in [their] waking up!" (Robinson 2).

Truman's problematic relationship with Meridian speaks to a larger issue within what is defined in *Black Feminist Thought* as Black "sexual politics" (Collins 153). Truman, like men who exist(ed) outside of the novel attempts to define himself within the constructs of a patriarchal system which has systematically denied African unity, community building, and cultural appreciation of the Black family. To quote Collins once more:

> African-American women have long commented on [the] 'love and trouble' tradition in Black women's relationships with Black men . . . Understanding this love and trouble tradition requires assessing the influence of heterosexist, Eurocentric gender ideology—particularly ideas about men and women advanced by the traditional family ideal—on African-American women and men. Definitions of appropriate gender behavior for Black women, Black men, and members of other racial/ethnic groups not only affect social institutions such as schools and labor markets; they also shape daily interactions (Collins 152–153).

After his estranged wife Lynne (one of the exchange students) accuses him of being a fraud and leaving her "as soon as black became beautiful," Truman reflects on his past actions. He has to decide if he is merely hiding behind a rhetorical fence—a wall of words and phrases that made him popular in the moment, but has no weight in the grand scheme of his life—or if he is truly prepared to accept the challenges of the Black community. Like that of the "new" Black middle class, *his* participation in the political process has been to adopt one fad after another. During this period of his youth, he remains a reluctant soldier, fighting for and against the systems that allow him to exist unobstructed. His intentions are unclear and he wrestles with the realities of obligation and self-preservation. As a college educated Black male he is obligated to solve problems of the Black community, but his education affords him a privilege that could eventually allow him to disengage from that same community.

In the events that frame the novel, Truman faithfully searches for Meridian and continues to be drawn toward her inner light, as well as her passion for the community hoping to understand his own purpose. For example, as a well-worn adult, on one of his familiar post-Civil Rights era sojourns to the south, Truman arrives in the town of Chicokema. He finds crowds of people gathered around a frail Meridian who is "staring down" a large army tank purchased during the 1960s in an effort to ward off the invasion of Northern liberals into the South. She is attempting to integrate a small shrine that houses the body of Marilene O'Shay, a woman murdered for adultery. When Truman asks a Black man (only identified as "the sweeper") about the incident, it is evident that they both fail to understand the true import of the situation. The dialogue is as follows:

(**Truman**): "What's happening?" he asked, walking up to an old man who was bent carefully and still as a bird over his wide broom."

(**Sweeper**): "Well . . . some of the children wanted to get in to see the dead lady, you know, the mummy woman, in the trailer over there, and our day for seeing her ain't until Thursday."

(**Truman**): "*Your* day?"

(**Sweeper**): "That's what I said."

(**Truman**): "But the Civil Rights Movement changed all that!"

(**Sweeper**): "I seen rights come and I seen 'em go . . . You're a stranger here or you'd know this is for the folks that work in that guano plant outside town. "*Po'folks*" (3–4) (bold emphasis mine).

Later in the same scene after Meridian successfully integrates the "museum," the sweeper exclaims, " . . . as far as I'm concerned. The stuff she do don't make no sense" (6–7). Truman's surprise at the continued need for activism in the Southern community represents his own ignorance of the community's changing needs. Not only do the struggles continue on account of race, but have continued to address oppression in all forms including child labor and exploitation of the poor. Although the majority of the children eager to see O'Shay's[5] decomposed body are Black, the sweeper makes a note to inform Truman of their common abject poverty rather than their race, by referring to their employment in the "guano plant."[6] Through the sweeper's dialogue with Truman it is apparent that the children are forced to work in deplorable and inhumane conditions. They, like children in "sweatshops" in developing countries are paid below living wage to produce fertilizer that ensures the agricultural (read: economical) progress of the South. Therefore, for these residents of Chicokema, the only thing   the Civil Rights movement changed was the methods by which they are oppressed.

When Truman asks the sweeper if he also works in the plant, he replies that he used to, but he was laid off for being "too old." Meridian's small revolutionary act can be read as being for "po' folks," Black folks, *and* old folks. By expanding her mission to include various oppressed groups she is able to live outside of the limitations of racism and exist within a metanarrative of holistic experience. Meridian's choice to remain in the South after the 1960s speaks to her continued service to the masses. She mobilizes as a method of combating the realities of unequal education, the exploitation of labor, and racism—all factors that do not affect her directly as an educated woman born into a middle class home, but affect her as a human.

After witnessing Meridian's standoff with the Chicokema police force, Truman mutters, "Now they will burst into song," in reference to the onlookers. But, the narrator adds, "They did not." It is evident at this point that Truman remains tied to a romanticized ideal of participatory action. He remembers the Negro spirituals accompanied by peaceful protest, small victories won, and a youthful idealistic notion of racial egalitarianism within a truly pluralistic society. He believes he can predict the singing, because the singing had always been there in the past—as a salve for the wounds of hate. But when the songs do not come, he is left silent, watching as Meridian's power is fueled by the latent energy of the community; a community that he feels, at this point, is unnecessary to save. It is not until Truman is stripped of all his "possessions" (wife, child, love, art) and returns to Meridian this last time that he begins to understand his power, and greater contribution to the communities. In the end, he rejects the trappings of middle-class sensibility as he undergoes a psychic transformation and finds himself contemplating his own future through the experiences of the rural folk.

"And in the darkness maybe we will know the truth."

–Meridian Hill

Just as Truman's actions and beliefs represent the flight(iness) of the Black middle class, Meridian embodies a self-sacrificing determination to serve the masses, at all costs. I read Meridian's continued support of the community as representative of the *Afro-Politico Womanist* agenda. APW as a standpoint theory supports a transformative Black community based on social, cultural, and political participation in world societies. In order for progress and significant change to occur, the entire community must be healthy. This includes access to health care (including holistic, spiritual, and traditional), emotional and mental healing, communication, and solidarity. This theoretical framework is a nationalist concept as it positions the needs, beliefs and survival of the Black community as the first priority.

As with Truman, Meridian exists in the novel in relation to those around her, but she does so as an Afro-Politico Womanist, in opposition to Truman's ambiguity. Though she considers herself alone, her solitude is enforced only by the mis-readings of her as "crazy" by the larger community. From childhood to her adult life, she does not fit into her mother's conservative Black community; rather she is a spiritual composite of Black experience. As a result, her dedication to the "cause" is more than a racial duty; it is the reason for her entire existence. Meridian views the fight, struggle, and battle of the 1960s as more than the demand for equality by brave soldiers. Early on, she recognizes the fallacy in supporting a rhetorical challenge to kill another person in the name of the "revolution," and instead uses her knowledge of Black experience and Black thought-processes to engage in unarmed offensive grass-roots support of the Black community. She resides in the communities, goes door-to-door asking illiterate heads of households to register to vote long after the freedom buses have pulled away, and still listens to their life stories when they refuse her offer. Meridian does not consider her undying loyalty to the rural Black south "revolutionary;" neither does she consider it a passing phase. The South is her home. When Truman tells Meridian that he grieves for the past, their loss, and the community's losses, in a "different" way than she does, she cannot accept his grief, because she does not see the death of her dreams.

Though Meridian spends her entire adult life debating the right answer to the question, "Will you kill for the revolution?," in the end she realizes that in order for the revolution to continue, real revolutionaries must live and ensure the survival of others as well. In "Double Jeopardy: To Be Black and Female" (1970), Frances Beale writes:

> We must begin to understand that a revolution entails not only the willingness to lay our lives on the firing line and get killed. In some ways, this is an easy commitment to make. To die for the revolution is a one-shot deal; to live for the revolution means taking on the more difficult commitment of changing our day-to-day life patterns (Beale 99).

As someone who has dedicated her life to living and fighting for the Black community, Meridian has refused to surrender. Her refusal to surrender is a spiritual act, as she becomes more empowered by her commitment to the community. Meridian's femme-centered choices are in direct contrast to the ideological shifts that Truman embraces. Truman accepts leadership roles, asserts his masculinity through sexual conquests, adapts to the shifting social and political scenes, and understands the Movement as being "over." Contrarily, Meridian works as a member of the community, refuses to surrender her body to the sexual gratification/pleasure of others, refuses an invitation into the Black middle class, and *knows* movements are incessant processes. Still, none of these acts or realizations can deter her from grass-roots activism.

Though Meridian remains in poor, rural communities as a worker, she does not adopt a traditional leadership role. Whereas, the other (male) characters active in the movement mobilize in very structured and institutionalized ways (producing pamphlets, speaking to the news media, organizing voter registration drives, and so forth), Meridian is primarily a doer, unattached to a specific organization or leader. This is significant when one considers the historical roles Black women have assumed in the fight for equality and justice. As noted previously, women like Ella Baker, Fannie Lou Hamer, and Bernice Johnson Reagon, were organizers and leaders behind the scenes, with disregard for an unhealthy emphasis on leadership. Baker's infamous quote, "strong people don't need strong leaders," is in reference to the adulation many Black ministers received during the Civil Rights Movement as the focus shifted from the poor to the educated elite. In *Political Process and the Development of Black Insurgency, 1930–1970*, Doug McAdam defines "leadership" as a "resource whose availability is conditioned by the degree of organization within the aggrieved population" (McAdam 48). He argues that without an organizational foundation (and/or the presence of leadership) indigenous groups are more likely to be "deprived of the capacity for collective action even when confronted with a favorable structure of political opportunities" (48). What McAdam and like theorists fail to take into consideration is organic grass-roots community work functioning outside the scope of a traditional organizational structure.

Meridian refuses the system in other ways, the most significant being her refusal to feel anything other than a visceral connection to human suffering. Her rejection of sexuality and romantic love manifests in her body's inability to succumb to pleasure. As a young woman she allows men to fondle her and engage in sexual intercourse, despite her mother's cryptic warnings to "be sweet," and not "be fast," but she does not ever allow them to define what should bring her to ecstasy (86). Her young lovers question her disposition by asking, 'Why are you always so sourfaced about it?' or later beg her not to tighten her muscles and lock her limbs, "this time" (55). Regardless of their urgings, the reader learns that Meridian's body does not allow her to give them into their desires:

> For as much as she wanted to, she—her body, that is—never had any
> intention of *giving in*. She was suspicious of pleasure. She might approach
> it, might gaze on it with longing, but retreat was inevitable (64).

Meridian is unable to experience a heightened physical state with her male
suitors (including Truman), or even her young husband, because her passion lies elsewhere. Society instructs that for a woman to experience pure
passion and orgasmic pleasure, she has to surrender her body to another
person, a (un)truth Meridian is not willing to accept. For it is important to
note that the times when Meridian does "feel," it is always connected to
a deeper understanding of ancestral ties or the love of the Black community—and only then does her mind release its tight grasp on her body.

For example, when Meridian enters into the "Sacred Serpent," an
Indian burial mound on her father's land, she experiences an ecstasy that
is unparalleled until she becomes a part of the Civil Rights Movement.
Meridian goes to the mound to "understand" the history of her great-
grandmother, Feather Mae, who had a life-changing experience in the pit of
the mound. For Meridian, Feather Mae stands as an exemplar of free-spir-
ited womanhood, living for pure pleasure and "denouncing all religion that
was not based on the experience of physical ecstasy" (51). When Meridian
enters the pit of the mound, she understands what it means to be alive:

> From a spot at the back of her left leg there began a stinging sensa-
> tion . . . Then her right palm, and her left, began to feel as if some-
> one had slapped them. But it was in her head that the lightness started.
> It was as if the walls of the earth that enclosed her rushed outward, lev-
> eling themselves at a dizzying rate, and then spinning wildly, lifting her
> out of her body and giving her the feeling of flying. And in this move-
> ment she saw the faces of her family, the branches of trees, the wings of
> birds, the corners of houses, blades of grass and petals of flowers rush
> toward a central point high above her and she was drawn with them, as
> whirling, as bright, as free, as they (52–53).

After she joins the Civil Rights Movement, Meridian is in a constant state
of heightened sensibility. Everything around her is tangible, and she soaks
up the pain, hurt, and hope of the community until she is emotionally
spent. She is described as "always in a state of constant tears," followed by
"the shaking of her hands, or the twitch in her left eye" (82). Both experiences, the mound and her physical response to joining the Movement,
place Meridian in a realm that cannot be satisfied by mere sexual gratifica-
tion. She experiences the mound *before* she becomes sexually active and

the Civil Rights Movement after she has married and given birth to her son. Neither of these traditionally "gratifying" experiences (sex and motherhood) can compare to Meridian's emotional passion for collective action. Her body rejects prescribed roles and she eventually gives her infant son away because she cannot give him the love he deserves. In turn, she accepts her self-sacrifice for humanity, social order, and communal love as the true route to her sensual power.

Another way Meridian remains connected to the masses is her rejection of the Black middle class. Through a scholarship given by a northern white philanthropist, Meridian is able to attend Saxon College, a historically Black women's college in Atlanta, Georgia (read: Spelman College). The university prides itself on its furtherance of bourgeois Victorian-era moral attitudes and a fine classical Liberal Arts education, though it is physically located in the heart of the poor and working class Black community. Saxon women are "as pure as the driven snow," and do not stray from the predictable path of virtue and propriety. The Saxon woman is not unlike Barbara Welter's description of the nineteenth-century "Cult of True Womanhood," a class of attributes ascribed to white virtuous women that is later adopted by the Black elite at the turn of the 20th century. Within the "Cult" the four main attributes, purity, piety, domesticity, and submissiveness, define Victorian-era womanhood and therefore, define the woman's "place" in the home and society (Carby 25).

Meridian is situated as an outsider upon first setting foot on the campus. She is no longer married, has given away her child, questions the existence of God, and continues to be active in the dirty job of liberation. In a school assembly Meridian speaks of her conflicting feelings about what she is supposed to believe and what she feels:

> [A]ll Saxon students were required to attend a chapel service at which one girl was expected to get up on the platform and tell—in a ten-minute speech—of some way in which she had resisted evil and come out on the right side of God. Meridian . . . did not believe she now stood even in the vicinity of God. In fact, Meridian was not sure there was a God, and when her turn came, she said so. . . . When her fellow students found themselves near her afterward they would look about as if they expected lightning to strike, and her teachers let her know she was a willful, sinful girl (93).

In *Reconstructing Womanhood*, Hazel Carby analyzes the problematic tensions that are present within the "Cult of True Womanhood,"—specifically as these tensions reflect the apparent powerlessness of Black (slave) women to be considered human, let alone women. One example includes a quote from Barbara Welter on the qualities of womanhood: "purity was as essential as piety . . . its absence as unnatural and unfeminine. Without it she was, in fact, no woman at all, but a member of some lower order" (Carby 25). Carby notes that the attributes reflect a social construction not developed with Black women in mind. Likewise, the social order at Saxon College is patterned after the upper-middle class bourgeois values of its white benefactors.

Historically, Black Colleges and Universities within this tradition (whether single-gender or co-ed) supported an education of propriety, religious teaching, class, and decorum which was instituted to produce ladies and gentlemen to society. Beneath the surface, the mission was more importantly to erase memories of slavery, ignorance, and the assumed inferiority of the Negro from American consciousness. Although negative images of Black Americans prevailed in the media and general populous, the education at Black colleges and universities ensured that students would situate themselves on the correct side (or the moral side), of the issues. The troubling aspects of this preventative action are the racial and cultural omissions, that would otherwise enable students to venture forth armed with historical memory and knowledge of America's indifferent attitude toward the Black community, as well as the perseverance and achievements of the race.[7] In "'Somebody Forgot to Tell Somebody Something': African-American Women's Historical Novels," Barbara Christian quotes Toni Morrison as she explains some of the reasons behind the silence:

> The title of my essay is taken from a radio interview Ntozake Shange did with Toni Morrison in 1978 . . . Morrison's comment referred to a generation of Afro-Americans of the post-World War II era who had seen the new possibilities that period seemed to promise for their children and who thought that knowledge of their history—one of enslavement, disenfranchisement, and racism—might deter the younger generation's hopes for the future" (Christian 220).

Unlike many of her counterparts at Saxon, Meridian *does* understand her history and the collective history of Black people locally and globally. It is precisely this knowledge that drives her "hopes for the future." In direct opposition to the constraints of the university's value system, it is at Saxon when Meridian fully immerses herself in the "Movement" and the plight of the poor Black community that surrounds the hallowed walls of the university campus. She comments on the irony of the gates that "keep the women in and the community out." Through her depiction of Meridian's defiance of institutional norms, Alice Walker openly critiques the historically Black colleges and universities that believe the liberation of its students is achieved through a classical education, and not communalism or collaboration with the Black masses.

Once she leaves Saxon, Meridian's decision to refuse traditional route(s) prescribed for her by others (because she is young, Black and female) leads to a conscious choice to live according an alternate set of rules. In the midst of racial turmoil and social upheaval Meridian remains still. Her refusal to merge into the pulse of the crowd and/or the trappings of convenient revolutionary rhetoric allows her to stand alone and acknowledge the cries and songs of the Black community. She envisions herself as a liberator—a constant force within the chaos of the masses. In the following passage, Meridian contemplates her role within the struggle:

> I am not to belong to the future. I am to be left, listening to the old music, beside the highway. But then, [she thought,] perhaps it will be my part to walk behind the real revolutionaries—those who know they must spill blood in order to help the poor and the black and therefore go right ahead—and when they stop to wash off the blood and find their throats too choked with the smell of murdered flesh to sing, I will come forward and sing from memory songs they will need once more to hear. For it is the song of the people, transformed by the experiences of each generation, that holds them together, and if any part of it is lost the people suffer and are without soul (221).

Meridian recognizes that her continued action is a product of her appreciation of Black historical memory. She has a spiritual connection to the people whom she asks to register to vote, those who risk their lives in the name of survival. Walker uses Meridian's life to show how history repeats itself through ancestral memory and collective action. Meridian absorbs the stories, songs, feelings, and pain of those in the struggle and uses that energy to continue voter registration drives, feed the poverty-stricken, listen to the stories, and live among those whom (Black middle class) society has forgotten. Walker's use of memory in the novel speaks to a larger cultural tradition involving black women's community and coalition building. In an essay on the black female literary tradition, Lorraine Bethel pronounces,

> . . . Black women have a long tradition of bonding together in a community that has been a source of survival information, and psychic and emotional support. We have a distinct Black woman-identified folk culture based on our experiences in society . . . this

Black woman-identified bonding and folk culture have often gone unrecorded except through our individual lives and memories (Bethel 179).

Meridian (both character and novel) represents the power of "bonding" and "folk culture," within the scope of Black activism. She remains within the community and celebrates everyday victories as well as defeats. Her encouragement is not limited to voting rights, clean facilities, and the occasional segregated "museum." What Meridian proves to the communities in which she lives and wanderers like Truman, is that humanity is the true testament of strength. Like the memories that bind Black culture together, true activists understand the "ethic of personal accountability" which connects each one to another through experience and shared circumstance.

As a Civil Rights novel, *Meridian* charts a path as an utopian text and the novel's ending speaks to the need for continuance—ongoing collective action and support within the Black community. When Truman returns to Meridian for the final time, she acknowledges *his* purpose and charges him with taking up the torch. She leaves him to contemplate his ability as a representative of the Black middle class to aid in the *real* revolution—this being the economic and social struggles of the next decade (1980s). Walker writes of Truman's ultimate transformation and decision to move back to the rural south:

> Truman turned, tears burning his face, and began, almost blindly to read the poems she had left on the walls. He could not bring himself to read the letters yet. It was his house now, after all. His cell. Tomorrow the people would come and bring him food. Someone would come milk his cow. They would wait patiently for him to perform, to take them along the next guideless step. Perhaps he would (Walker 242).

Several scholars contend that Meridian's departure at the end of the novel is symbolic of death—the death of the Civil Rights movement and Meridian's own death due to her failing health. Others read her exit as the passing of the torch, the task of salvation going from one champion of the community to another. Yet others read the final scene as "no reason to believe that Meridian's change has catalyzed, or been abled by, a corresponding transformation of her social and political context" (143–44 Dubey).

While there are many possible interpretations of the ending, *Meridian's* strength is its ability to imagine continuation and social change, especially as it is connected to the hopeful return of a prodigal middle class. In the last scene Truman's thoughts, emotions, and physical actions end the novel. Walker writes that Truman was not concerned with either the traditionalists who "gnash their teeth" at Meridian's behavior or the revolutionists who will "deplore [her] ambivalence" adding "Truman . . . was not himself concerned about either group. To him they were practically imaginary" (242). Truman realizes his own humanity outside of organizational structures and limitations. The revolutionists and traditionalists are now "imaginary" to him, where before they defined his actions. In actuality, the organizations that Meridian and Truman reject are "imaginary" existing only for the moment and dissipating after the chains of exclusion have been broken. Symbolically, Truman represents the necessity of a Black middle class return to the masses and the need to continue unfinished business.

Chapter Four

"Ain't No Such Animal as an Instant Guerilla"

Composing Self and Community in Toni Cade Bambara's *The Salt Eaters*

> . . . Instant coffee is the hallmark of the current rhetoric. But we do have time. We'd better take the time to fashion revolutionary selves, revolutionary lives, revolutionary relationships . . . Ain't no such animal as an instant guerilla.
>
> —Toni Cade, 1969

Several comparisons exist between Alice Walker's *Meridian* (1976) and Toni Cade Bambara's *The Salt Eaters* (1980), as texts that examine the continuity of Black women's activism after the "official" end to the Civil Rights and Black Power movements. For example, in *The Salt Eaters* (*TSE*), when Minnie Ransom, the town's "fabled healer" asks Velma Henry, a weary champion of social justice, "Are you sure, sweetheart, that you want to be *well*," the reader can easily recall Meridian Hill and her quest for healing. At the start of *Meridian*, Truman Held (a former lover and colleague) also questions Meridian's health after witnessing her successful attempt to integrate a local carnivalesque exhibit, on behalf of a group of economically disadvantaged children. She is visibly weak, loses consciousness for periods of time, and wears a conductor's cap to conceal her hair loss. She replies to Truman's questioning, "Of course I'm sick. Why do you think I spend all this time trying to get *well*!" (Walker 10, emphasis mine).

What is significant about both texts is the inseparable link between community and individual health. Both women are at the physical end of a self-sacrificing quest to rescue the Black community from racism, classism, sexism, and even itself, as the dawning of a new era approaches. In the process, Meridian participates in a vicious corporeal tug-of-war that leads to bouts of spiritual "sickness." Her refusal to surrender her mind, body, or soul to the world outside the plight of the poor, precipitates the breakdown of her very essence. Like Meridian, Velma Henry is self-destructive in her love and devotion to the Black community, but this devotion has a

59

dangerous outcome: her revolutionary solution to the weight of the struggle results in attempted suicide. In the end, both women are transformed through renewal processes and individual revolutions, as they realize that they must live and be well to ensure continued social activism on behalf of the community.

Against *Meridian* and the presence of historical Black female activism, *TSE* acts as what Henry Louis Gates, Jr. defines as a signifying text. In *The Signifying Monkey* (1988) Gates explains:

> Much of the Afro-American literary tradition can be read as successive attempts to create a new narrative space for representing the recurring referent of Afro-American literature, the so-called Black Experience . . . These relationships are reciprocal because we are free to read in critical time machines, to read backward, as Merlin moved through time.
>
> . . . It should be clear, even from a cursory familiarity with the texts of the Afro-American tradition, that black writers read and critique the texts of other black writers as an act of rhetorical self-definition. Our literary tradition exists because of these chartable formal relationships, relationships of Signifyin(g) (Gates 111, 122)

The "chartable formal relationship" that Gates posits between Black writers exists as an exploration of ways to "save" and heal the unhealthy Black masses, in Bambara's and Walker's novels. Both novels examine the lives of individual women and the impact their strength has on the community. Through their relationships with others and ultimate spiritual breakthroughs, Meridian Hill and Velma Henry understand their positions as torchbearers in the race for collective salvation. *Meridian* acknowledges the flight of the Black middle class from the poor and working class communities as the source of pain and distrust among members of rural southern communities "left over" from the media attention to Civil Rights during the 1960s.

In *Healing Narratives: Women Writers Curing Cultural Dis-Ease*, Gay Wilentz "examine[s] women writers from diverse ethnic backgrounds as cultural workers who aim, through their writings, to heal self and community from these socially constructed diseases" (Wilentz 3). For Wilentz, Velma's move from mental instability to "wellness" is possible through the acceptance of African healing practices and cultural traditions. Likewise, though her examination of Minnie Ransom, she explores the "role of woman as healer to cure cultural dis-ease" (3). Wilentz's reading of healing in the novel is useful when thinking about representations of community-based Black political action during what scholars view as the waning years of Black community growth and progress (1970–1980).

The theme of reconnecting with an African based spirituality and traditional way of life that point to communalism and community preservation runs throughout the novel. As cultural nationalists believe that reflection and acceptance of an African past is the only true form of liberation, Bambara argues for a holistic reassessment of the Black community that will confront the current confused state and channel the peoples' aimless behavior into a common freedom movement. I argue that *TSE* uses Velma's own reinvention to signify the necessary reformulation of these fragmented selves.

TSE provides a space to consider massive Black cultural restoration as the next step in revolutionary community activism. The novel accepts what other texts suggest—that the connection between a spiritual and political self will decide the outcome of the future. Though the fictional residents of Claybourne, Georgia have witnessed organizational decline, gender biases, and the failures of community-based coalitions, through Velma Henry's regeneration process Bambara provides an alternative to a moribund future. Members of the community define Velma as a wife, mother, goddaughter, sister, spy, organizer, activist, anarchist, and finally, a mentally imbalanced victim of disillusionment and frustration. As Velma breaks through her shell of instability and disbelief, her consciousness-raising experience as she struggles to become whole renews her strength and determination to fight for the community.

This chapter examines the relationship between Claybourne and the impending destruction of the larger Black community through representations of gender bias within organizations, dysfunctional relationships, and failed coalition building. While the novel centers on Velma's attempted suicide and the choices she must make to "be well" in the end, Velma's regeneration becomes Bambara's remedy for a heartbroken community on the cusp of a new decade.

As I have argued, organizational strength and gender politics are variables that factor into examination of APW being a viable strategy for the reclamation and salvation of the Black community. *TSE*, as an *Afro-Politico Womanist* novel, speaks to a growing concern in the late 1970s for the fate of the Black community as a new decade approached. Among other things, Bambara explores the possible dangerous outcomes for a community "excus[ing] the self from the chaos of the moment, looking for a past or for a future as if there were no continuum, and no real threat that energized and carried one" (Bambara 98). As a narrative that addresses

mental fatigue and hopelessness, the novel provides a remedy for the fledg-
ling fictional community that is representative of challenges facing a highly
individualistic post-Civil Rights generation. The residents of Claybourne,
Georgia are still reeling from a decade of violence, broken promises, and
collective death, but refuse to gravitate toward each other. This lack of connection surfaces as broken relationships between Black men and women in
the community, similar to the "psychological problems" Beale describes in
"Double Jeopardy," which result from the inability for Black men to find
employment and support their families, as well as an increased emphasis on
masculine ideals and traditional gender roles (Beale 90).

Here Bambara critiques the poorly derived strategies for community building when organizations employed men at the helm and women
"behind the scenes." This formation became problematized when Black
women chose to redefine their experiences from within and previously
"silent"[1] women spoke up and out for what they saw as the destructive
impact faulty leadership had on the Black community. The novel, like APW
does not support the creation and/or reliance upon organizations with top-
down leadership, thereby acknowledging the rise of Black women's collec-
tives as a response to hierarchical plans of community action.

The novel enters into a longstanding discussion of Black women in
the Black revolution. Whereas before theorists, novelists, activists, and
writers discussed the roles Black women would "play," at the time *TSE* is
written (1978–1980) the conversation has shifted to address the formation
of separate women's alliances, female subjugation, and domestic violence
within the Black community. Works like *The Third Life of Grange Copeland* (Walker); *for colored girls who have considered suicide when the rain-
bow is enuf* (Shange); *Corregidora* (Jones); *Eva's Man* (Jones); *Sister X and
the Victims of Foul Play* (Polite); *Black Macho and the Myth of the Superwoman* (Wallace) and so forth, contributed to a larger social/political discussion of the Black woman as sexualized and racialized within particular
struggles. In her 1970 essay, "Double Jeopardy: To Be Black and Female,"
Frances Beale examines the subaltern position of the Black woman within
American society.[2] As a racialized "Other," she is unable to benefit from the
same rights and privileges as her white counterparts. Similarly, as a woman
she is relegated to the last rung of the economic ladder, the result being less
pay for comparable work and disrespect at work and home. Beale writes,

> The economic system of capitalism finds it expedient to reduce women
> to a state of enslavement. They oftentimes serve as a scapegoat for the
> evils of this system . . . so, by giving to men a false feeling of superi-
> ority (at least in their own home or in their relationships with women),

the oppression of women acts as an escape valve for capitalism. Men may be cruelly exploited and subjected to all sorts of dehumanizing tactics on the part of the ruling class, but they have someone who is below them—at least they're not women (Beale 94).

Similar to the novelists mentioned above, Black women's consciousness-raising groups engaged in sociological studies and compiled information that spoke to an increasing need to consider the Black woman's position in the future of the community. Like APW, these groups considered the various factors that influence Black women's community involvement and the multiple struggles that need to be addressed to ensure a healthy community. Examples include The Combahee River Collective; Patricia Robinson and Group; Adele Jones and Group; and the Black Women's Community Development Foundation.

> *The men smoked and drummed their fingers on the tabletop and*
> *the women went on writing . . .*
>
> *-The Salt Eaters*

In the novel, what appear as a series of dream sequences are actually flashbacks that represent the chaos that has brought Velma to her breaking point. Within this mélange of memories the reader learns that Velma harbors pain and anger from a past riddled with female self-sacrifice resulting from stratagems that advance male leadership in the community. Velma recalls the sacrifices she makes for "the cause":

> Like going to jail and being forgotten, forgotten, or at least deprioritized cause bail was not as pressing as the printer's bill. Like raising funds and selling some fool to the community with his heart set on running for public office. Like being called in on five-minute notice after all the interesting decisions had been made, called in out of personal loyalty and expected to break her hump pulling off what the men had decided was crucial for the community good (Bambara 25).

Velma recalls the allowances she made, not as a method of boasting or a call for retribution, but as the impetus for the near fatal act that has placed her in the infirmary. The theme of "too much to bear" runs throughout the novel and is attributed to the weight female activists and organizers carried behind the scenes. Like Velma, women organizers during the Black Power movement initially agreed that Black men "should be given more leadership and responsibility," but understood that behind the rhetoric men had a long way to go before they would be able to participate in all aspects (Fleming 206).

Bambara presents the umbrella community organization Velma is a member of as one that includes men and women representing "colleagues, chums, frat brothers, soror sisters, business partners, co-workers, neighbors" (Bambara 28). The members are representative of groups indigenous to the Black community that have historical roots in the uplift of the Black race and community action. According to sociologist Aldon Morris, "mass protest is the product of the organizing efforts of activists functioning through a well-developed indigenous base" (Morris xii). This base includes all aspects of the community (money, churches, organizations, leaders, etc.) from which social movements can be created and fostered.

The "indigenous resources" are then transformed into resources of power and political strength that provide the foundation for organizational growth (xii). In the novel, when a "visitor" from the "Coalition of Black Trade Unionists" addresses the group, the women in the room exhibit their positions as indigenous resources as they ensure the organization's growth and balance. Bambara writes,

> Once again the women took up their pens. They listened to Hampden while calculating: money to be raised, mailing lists to be culled, halls to be booked, flyers to be printed up, hours away from school, home, work, sleep to be snatched. Not that he spoke of these things.

And later,

> And while he urged them to grasp the significance of new alliances shaping up against the Carter administration, the men smoked and drummed their fingers on the tabletop and the women went on writing: so many receptions to cater, tickets to print, chickens to fry, cakes to box, posters to press . . . (Bambara 27)

Through her representations of women's behind the scenes work, Bambara critiques Black organizations designed to bolster the public face of Black male leadership while taking for granted the work that is necessary to support the organization from the ground up. The women understand the real work that has to continue whether or not alliances are formed with other organizations. Later in the same meeting, when the women rebel against the male leadership, it is Velma's responsibility to vocalize why the usual "pattern" (women doing all the work why the men sit by and stare) has to change. She speaks,

And we have yet to see any of you so much as roll up your sleeves to empty an ashtray . . . Do you have a grant for one of us? Any government contracts? Any no-work-all-pay posts at a college, those of you on boards? . . . We shuttle back and forth to the airport, yawl drink at the bar. We caucus, vote, lay out the resolutions, yawl drink at the bar. We're trying to build a union, a guild, an organization. You are all welcome to continue operating as a social club, but not on our time, okay? (37).

In an act of desperation and frustration, Velma and the newly formed "Women for Action" find it necessary to establish their own organization separate from the men who are not seriously invested in the plight of the Black community. The choice to break from the larger collective speaks to the continued support Black women give the community within and outside of a time of crisis. As noted previously, continued activism often requires women to distance themselves from the egotistical battles between male "leaders" who remain more invested in their own causes than in the community's welfare. As Velma remembers these moments she continues to internalize the rupture between the male and female "workers" and stands somewhere in between trying to hold the pieces together.

In addition to exposing ills related to the failure of organizational solidarity, Bambara also references the connections between male/female relationships and the dangerous influence of capitalism and public policy. The ability of discriminatory and racialized government policies to disrupt the lives of its "minority" citizens exists as another topic of contention that contributes to disruptive gender relationships in the novel. Through the exploration of gender politics and the lower class community, Bambara addresses increased numbers of Black women on the welfare payroll, and the stigmatization of the Black welfare mother including illegitimacy, and dysfunctional relationships. She explores these weighty issues through the character of Meadows, a university trained medical specialist interning in Claybourne. As an outsider to the community, he becomes increasingly aware that his social and class difference place him on the opposite side of the Black underclass. He is described as a fair-skinned Black man, having "red-gold hair of no less than five grades—curly in front, stringy in back, wavy around the ears, slick on top, and downright nappy in the center" (186). He realizes that he is "never more clear to himself than when Black people examined him" (186).

As he moves throughout the community he becomes increasingly aware that it is his social and class difference that forever places him on the opposite side of the Black underclass—not his skin color. As he notices his surroundings he observes the poverty and desolation that engulf the particular section of the community in which he has wandered. On his journey of contemplation, observation, and reflection he encounters several inhabitants of the neighborhood and immediately considers his temporary presence in this new locale as juxtaposed with their everyday realities. He sees a woman wearing a housecoat, barking dogs, the hulls of abandoned cars, and realizes that he has entered into a world from his distant past:

> This was evidently where the poorer people lived. There were broken-down stoops that looked like city and leaning porches that looked like country. Houses with falling-away shutters and brick walkways that wouldn't make up their minds. Claybourne hadn't settled on its identity yet, he decided. Its history put it neither on this nor that side of the Mason Dixon. And its present seemed to be a cross between a little Atlanta, a big mount Bayou and Trenton, New Jersey, in winter (Bambara 181).

Meadows eyes the streets, homes, and people with a trained ethnographic eye, a participant observer who is separated from the fate of those around him by class and culture while simultaneously vying to be accepted within Black culture. Noting that "the block [was] so like his first a hundred lives ago," he at the same time acknowledges his disgust at the pathologies within the Black community that allowed his memories of poverty to remain so vivid.

As Meadows hurries down the street he notes "a dark-skinned man with a cap yanked low over an unruly bush." He quickly classifies him as a "welfare man," the men who made their living benefiting from mothers on welfare (182). The reader learns that Meadows "had seen them, made a study of them, knew the look, the posture," and as a result of his "studies" he abhors their presence and emasculated irresponsibility. The presence of these men in the supermarkets disturb Meadows "because the women were there, there and losing. And because he was there, there and helpless" (184). His observations reflect public debate on Black masculinity, poverty, and the plight of the lower-class Black family. As a public policy, welfare aids in the dependency on a system of supplemental income—typified as income male members of the household are unable to contribute. The men, according to Meadows, in turn depend on their female partners and exist as "boymen"—perpetual children enacting infantile and irresponsible behavior:

> In parks, on roofs, in bars, on stoops, but especially in supermarkets running their whining line while the women reached round them for a can of whatever was on sale. The boymen grabbing at their

pocketbooks or their arms and the women saying "Naw, man, gotta feed my kids . . .

. . . And by the time they got to the line and the welfare mamas were fishing out the coupons, worn out with all the haggling, the boymen would lean in for the kill, mashing their joints into the women, mashing the women into the shopping arts, the mesh outlined on ass or hips, the purses clutched so hard the vinyl tore. 'A dime, woman, a damn dime.' And the women, defeated would dip into the coins and give it up, then look over the items moving along the belt for the one thing the children might possibly do without (183).

When outlining the socio-political variables underlying Black women's fiction from this era, I identified the highly controversial (and widely read) 1965 report on the Black family compiled by then senator Patrick Moynihan (NY) as a source of problematic gender relationships within the Black community during the post-Civil Rights period. Because several Black leaders allowed the Black family to be defined from the outside, dangerous attitudes toward Black women surfaced and threatened unity within the larger community. In the infamous "Moynihan report," Patrick Moynihan contends that the "underlying cause of the rising welfare rolls, the increased poverty," and high rates of Black male unemployment is the reversed gender roles within the Black family (Crass 6). According to Moynihan, Black women are typically more educated and economically independent while their men remain dependent, uneducated and chronically unemployed. What results from this degenerate family structure are the emasculation of Black boys by the matriarch, the rejection of Black masculine "power," and the proliferation of female-headed households (6).

In a general sense, the connections Moynihan makes between poverty, welfare assistance, and the Black matriarch are illogical. For example, if Black woman are able to support their families as a result of higher education and employment in white-collar positions, as Moynihan posits, why is it necessary for these same women to receive public assistance? Or, if the increase in poverty (and federally funded "handouts") results from Black male depression and flight from their homes because of a domineering, economically independent female partner, why not institute policies that would address employment and education discrimination—the real root of the issue? Not only did the federally supported report bring national attention to the issues of poverty and dysfunction within the Black community, lawmakers were now able to shift the blame of rising AFDC[3] costs to a pathology of poverty and despair which the government should not be responsible for, in their opinion. In "Beyond Welfare Queens: developing a race, class, and gender analysis of Welfare and Welfare Reform," Chris Crass writes,

> Moynihan argued that the Black family was a tangled web of pathologies. Drug addiction, self-hate, violence, lack of work ethic, dependency, out-of-wedlock, illegitimate babies and the teen mothers who can't take care of themselves let alone a child. These pathologies are the result of the breakdown of the Black family (Crass 7).

The debates over who was to blame for all of the aforementioned issues (pathologies, costs, dysfunction) bled into the Black community and further alienated Black men and women within their relationships to each other. What Moynihan, his colleagues, and many members of the Black community failed to acknowledge was by the 1960s "only 16 percent of nonwhite unwed mothers received ADC compared with 30 percent of white women" (Levenstein 10). Conveniently, the branding of lower class Black women as "welfare queens"—highly promiscuous women who produce hoards of children and make *their* living as recipients of welfare, fit into the already established stereotypes regarding Black women in the larger society. Levenstein cites negative press as another contributor to already problematic perceptions of a luxurious life for Black female welfare recipients. She writes:

> Newspapers did not report that 28 percent of ADC households in 1960 lacked flush toilets and 17 percent had no running water. Instead, the media often portrayed life on welfare as so comfortable as to be addictive, failing to acknowledge that because of meager employment opportunities and government grants, at least one in seven ADC recipients also worked for wages outside the home (10).

The negative associations surrounding Black women's power, vulnerability, independence and dependence becomes the meeting place for white conservative backlash, federal debate, and slanderous statements made by Black leaders. Women are blamed for their abilities to qualify for welfare, have children, to be educated, or to be independent, while as Kay Lindsey observes, the government is the real culprit. She argues that "the state has created an artificial family, in which it, via the welfare check, takes the place of the husband and can thus manipulate the 'family' more directly" (Lindsey 88). The intimacy of a strong relationship is absent within this manufactured family and as Meadows observes, the men and women he encounters in the supermarket do not even refer to each other by name

(Bambara 185). They maintain a familiarity based on desperation and help-lessness, not unity.

Additional outside influences contribute to strained gender relations among the Black masses. Whereas Black educated middle-class men are able assert their authority in leadership positions within civic organizations in the community and are respected for their knowledge and income, lower-class males do not have the same privileges. Like Bigger Thomas in Richard Wright's *Native Son*, street credibility and reckless acts as a form of respect become an accessible outlet for internal rage and frustration. Overall, the ways in which men and women interact with each other become danger-ous and destructive for the health of the family and community structures. In "Is the Black Male Castrated?" Jean Carey Bond and Patricia Peery acknowledge the tumultuous relationships between Black men and women. They write:

> After all, the cat who sponges off of you, knocks you around every now and then, and maybe leaves you, is Black, not white. By the same token, the chick who tells you this is her money, she made it, and you can just get the hell out, is Black, not white. But we are, in fact, focus-ing only on the trees when we expend time and energy in this senseless and debilitating family squabble while the real culprits stand laughing in the wings (Bond and Peery 115).

What Bond and Peery identify is a Marx-influenced critique of the connec-tion between the state and female subjugation. The authors note the dam-age inflicted on interpersonal relationships when hegemonic ideology of the state oppresses male members of the proletariat. In turn, these members recreate acts of oppression and domination within the home, and as Ruby, another female character in *TSE* articulates, "all the unresolved stuff slops over into man/woman relationships" (Bambara 199).

> *"Scattered, fragmented, uncoordinated mess . . . and nothing changing"*
>
>   –Ruby

In the novel, as the women and men struggle through the challenges ahead, another area of contention that adds to Claybourne's chaos is the overall subsistence of the community. The attempts at reconstruction and progress are displayed by organization building, the embrace of tradition, incorporating nationalist ideologies into systems of community govern-ment, and the prevention of "big business" from infiltrating the small town.

Ironically, the various attempts to address the aforementioned issues lead to further disunity among community groups and members. Each organization wants its specific need met, leaving little room for coalition building and/or the collapsing of ideas under a larger umbrella cause. In a telling scene, Velma's husband Obie, who works at a community center called "the Academy" (7 Arts), makes observations about the reoccurring ideological schisms in the community. He notes:

> It was starting up again, the factions, the intrigue. A replay of all the old ideological splits: the street youth as vanguard, the workers as vanguard; self-determination in the Black Belt, Black rule of U.S.A.; strategic coalitions, independent political action. Camps were forming threatening to tear the Academy apart . . . The masseuse, karate master, the language teachers and the resident reggae band feeling more than estranged were asking, Whatever happened to Third World Solidarity? (90–91).

What Obie notes in the 1970s are familiar to him because the same issues resulted in disaster for the Black community in the 1960s. The fact that "it was starting up again" alludes to the revival of latent tensions between groups. Each groups' solution to the internal challenges is indicative of the "war of words" fought between Cultural and Revolutionary Nationalists. Each nationalist group believes their methods of action are the only way the Black masses will progress and prosper.

Instead of positioning nationalist discourse as primarily a function within one community, Bambara reflects the changing face of the nationalist question. Indeed, Obie considers the grass-roots work that needs to be done in the community and how the next move was to complete the work that the Lowndes County Freedom Party started,[4] and "mobilize the people to form and support a Black political party before it was too late" (91). But, in addition to the needs of the Blacks he also recognizes the connections that need to be made with similar political groups of color like the "Puerto Rican Nationalist Party," the La Raza Unida groups," "the American Indian Movement" along with a "loose, informal network of medicine people throughout the communities of color to be lifted up and formalized" (91). Obie's focus on coalition building reflects the changing politics of the era.

By 1970 certain revolutionary nationalist organizations recognized that the fight against oppression was a worldwide struggle for all people of color. During this period Third World scholars like Frantz Fanon were embraced for research on the psychological effects of colonization on colonized people. Also public outcry against the U.S. government-lead terrorism of the Vietnamese people, the defeat of the American military, and the subsequent ending of the Vietnam War, shone the light on worldwide oppression as a result of an existing capitalist paradigm. In *The Black Panthers Speak*, Phillip Foner outlines the Black Panther Party's aims of building a coalition between groups that address the needs of oppressed minorities. He notes that the Black Panther Party formed alliances with groups who modeled their community programs after the Party (Foner 219). Examples of these groups include the Puerto Rican "Young Lords;" the Chicano "Brown Berets;" the "Young Patriots" who focused on poor whites; and the Chinese-American "Red Guards" (Foner 219).

Unfortunately, what Obie and Velma face when trying to unite divergent factions in their home community and align them with similar groups, is a return to the pervasive "gender wars," and discontent among organizations internal to the Black community. They encounter heavy resistance on the part of "the Brotherhood," who are not eager or willing to allow the "Women of Action" to merge with their organization. The constant bickering and dissention among like factions results in a "Babel of paths, of plans" that hinders effective political mobilization and/or progress.

The "scattered" community is further represented through the warnings and wise words of the "elders" who work within the physical and spiritual realm to protect Velma from herself and also comment on the inevitable outcome of the chaotic community. As Minnie Ransom tries to bring Velma back from her self-imposed mental exile, she holds a psychic conversation with her spirit guide (Old Wife) that ends in a diatribe against the carelessness of the "new people," or present generation. Like an elder surveying the actions of her family, Minnie shakes her head at the "children" who threaten the sanctity of the Black community. She remarks,

> Soon's they old enough to start smelling theyselves, they commence to looking for blood amongst the blood. Cutting and stabbing and facing off an daring and dividing up and suiciding . . . Everybody all up in each other's face with a whole lotta who struck John—you ain't correct, well you ain't cute, and he ain't right and they ain't scientific and yo mama don't wear no drawers and get off my suedes, and he hit me, and she quit me, and this one's dirty, and that one don't have a degree, and on and on (Bambara 46).

Like those who subscribe to a postmodern ideal, the new breed of Black people is not invested in upholding the traditions and common goals that kept the Black community together in the past. In addition to people like Meadows, who have become removed from the plight of the Black community and can only observer from afar, the individuals that comprise the masses themselves are "looking for blood amongst the blood," and willing to destroy those around them to further independent and capitalistic goals. According to the elders in the novel, people have forgotten how to be whole and well and therefore, individuals cannot fully participate as part of a cultural unit—hence the insistence on self-destruction (107).

> *"In the last quarter, sweetheart, anything can happen. And will."*
>
> —Minnie Ransom

In the end, Velma Henry is the link that holds the novel together. Through her experiences, mental and physical depression, and unwillingness to bear the heavy burden of an ailing community, the reader sees her choice to survive within the larger context of an idealistic vision for the contemporary community. Velma's character is integral to the narrative because she embodies the Black activist whose own well-being is connected to the political strength of the masses. As an example of an Afro-Politico Womanist, Velma works tirelessly within the community and does not align herself with divided ideological camps. Her experiences fall between cultural nationalist beliefs in liberation through the embrace of African traditional healing and the emphasis on a political revolution that would restructure contemporary society. Velma's attempt at suicide provides a temporary release from a chaotic and disjointed community and allows her to reinvent herself and return whole:

> And in time Velma would find her way back to the roots of life. And in doing so, be a model. For she'd found a home amongst the community workers who called themselves 'political.' And she'd found a home amongst the workers who called themselves 'psychically adept.' But somehow she'd fallen into the chasm that divided the two camps. Maybe that was the lesson. Maybe the act of trying to sever a vein or climbing into the oven was like going to the caves, a beginning . . . (147–8).

Velma's physical and mental changes throughout the novel precede a defining moment in her life and the life of the community. As she struggles to find her way back and understand the reasons for her breakdown, the reader learns of the bouts of "madness" Minnie Ransom had before she realized her gift for spiritual healing. As a young woman, Minnie embarked on a spiritual journey those around her failed to understand. She was representative of the town's successes, an upstanding member of the community until she returned from the north "on the train lying down." Bambara writes, "They called her batty, fixed, possessed, crossed, in deep trouble . . . the sight of Minnie Ransom down on her knees eating dirt, craving pebbles and gravel, all asprawl in the road with her clothes every which way—it was too much to bear" (51). Eventually, Minnie realizes that it was *necessary* for her to shirk the materialism and manufactured traditions that defined her up to that point, in order to realize her true calling. Though others in the community believed her actions to be an omen of death or possession, Minnie finds that the process was about "a gift unfolding" (53). This gift is the power to heal those who have disconnected from the earth, traditions, and spirituality—the only method of remaining whole in a fragmented society.

Likewise, Velma experiences similar "fits of madness" before she slits her wrists and places her head in the oven in an attempt to silence the voices inside. She considers suicide the most viable method of escaping herself and the pressures of a community that does not want to save itself. Her husband (Obie) recalls her strange behavior before the attempted suicide,

> But *she* couldn't relax. Not Velma. Walking jags, talking jags, grabbing his arm suddenly and swirling her eyes around the room, or collapsing in the big chair, her head bent over . . . And at night, holding her, he felt as though he were holding on to the earth in a quake, the ground opening up, the trees toppling, the mountains crumbling, burying him (162).

What ultimately scares Velma (and Obie) is the same process that Minnie goes through as a young woman. The key to the earth shaking upset of her life is the gift unfolding—the ability to be a conduit of healing and salvation for the sick. As a community activist, Velma receives the gift so she will be well equipped to aid in her community's healing and growth as the "last quarter" of the era approaches. Like others in the community, she believed that the work she needed to do in the 1970s would be focused more on repairing the damage done to the Sixties generation. What she finds is that the theoretical solutions to the problems facing the Black community did not "take." "Time was running out anyhow" and the masses were spiraling toward a destructive reality that required a full-scale reinvention rather than simply damage repair (258).

As a novel of healing and self-reclamation, *TSE* suggests a remedy for a (fl)ailing southern community scarred by aborted liberation efforts and post-Civil Rights nihilism. It is significant that the novel is set in the American South, not only because of slavery's legacy and the connection to an African spiritual history, but also because the south as the point of first contact and contention is the logical region where healing must begin. The southern region as Promised Land and utopia in the 1970s was a prominent theme in many cultural and political deliberations on the site of a new Black revolution. In a 1970 essay titled "Looking Back" by Helen Cade Brehon she writes, "After looking back over the years I am certain that the greatest strides, the greatest changes, will be seen in the South. The people in the South have tolerated more, so they are more fed-up, disgusted, and will act" (Brehon 231). Helen Cade Brehon echoes hopeful and idealistic sentiments about the future of the "revolution" in the midst of uncertainty about positive change. In this vein, the fictional city of Claybourne can be read as representative of the collective healing that needs to take place in Black communities nationwide before further revolutionary practices can occur.

As a tireless political activist and champion of social justice, Velma Henry embodies the internal confusion of the community and fools herself into believing that the only viable solution is self-murder. However, as one of the physician's notes, her suicide "hadn't looked like a serious attempt anyway." Comparatively, what can be deemed the attempted suicide of the Black community during 1970–1980 was not "serious," but a desire to be rescued and much needed time to heal after the pain and wounds of the "movement years."

When those affected by social ills, tumultuous relationships, and general discontent within a capitalist, racist, and sexist context can compose themselves and return to the center—a true metamorphosis can occur. Black women writers during the rise of Postmodernism (and the fall of Black communalism) visualized a better tomorrow that would liberate their communities from pathological destruction and reconnect relationships. Through her current observations of troubled community organizing efforts and general anxiety about the coming era, Bambara anticipated a collective shedding of current evils as the horizon appeared, but understood that there are no instant solutions and that everyone must take a little revolutionary *time*.

Chapter Five

"Something That's Been Up Has to Come Down"

Global Black Consciousness in Paule Marshall's *The Chosen Place, The Timeless People*

> Africana women novelists are mediators, then, functioning liminally. As such, it is not surprising that their stories always feature travel, whether it is the nomadism of the postcolonial subject or the forced uprooting of the enslaved African, or both, in the case of the postcolonial Africana subject. More importantly, however, their stories feature the return trip . . . that allows for healing and the restoration of wholeness.
>
> —Nada Elia

The tenets of the *Afro-Politico Womanist* model suggest an understanding of the diverse approaches Black women activists have to community building, public policy, and education, within the realm of collective action. The fictional representations of Black women's work within and on behalf of the community speak to the existence of several feminist working groups during the post-Civil Rights era whose primary mission was to (re)claim the voice of marginalized "Third World" women. Generally, the "victim" was subaltern, restricted within conservative doctrinal values, (as with Middle Eastern Bedouin women and Kenyan Muslims), and she suffered from a lack of economic and political power. Often, the women charged with alleviating the pain of political oppression and chauvinism were white aid workers or feminist scholars whose goals included creating a sacred space for all women, regardless of national origin.

While the activists championing these larger projects were effective in affecting public policy and increasing international awareness of subjects ranging from slave labor to female circumcision, in many instances their presence in the spotlight assumed a lack of continuous grass-roots activity within the targeted community. In many cases, the platforms provided to outside agents did not allow those working on the inside to exist as anything more than exploited tokens of oppression, and/or the "face" of the problem. The lessons learned from this involvement proved for many that indigenous female subversive activity can become lost in various translations of poverty, sexism, and despair, when the experiences of the subaltern are not considered from the ground level upward.[1] Recently, several scholars have considered the consequences of the commercialization of struggles worldwide.[2] Others argue that various challenges like AIDS, poverty, genocide, and world hunger cannot be fought without the help of the West. While contemporary discussions are relevant and necessary, it is also important to consider a retrospective analysis of global activism. Reflecting on the initial conversations about the silencing of the oppressed requires us to reconsider the danger in defining activism from the outside, when participating in current movements for social change.

Now as before, the argument remains that the presence (or absence) of the indigenous voice must be examined before progress can be made. Within this vein, I find it useful to acknowledge the messages included in Africana women's fiction written in the post-Civil Rights era that depicts the Black postcolonial community in turmoil. Through their own experiential connection to the global Black community, the Diasporic authors critique the external gaze on the Black masses by the Black middle class, provide representations of attempts at betterment through internally defined political action, as well as examine gender politics in their respective communities. Works by female writers representing Africa, the Caribbean, and South America such as Buchi Emecheta (Nigeria), Ellen Kuzwayo (South Africa), Besse Head (South Africa), Erna Brodber (Jamaica), and Miriam Alves (Brazil) identify Black female circles of healing, progress, and change as the locus of freedom from hegemonic superstructures that work within a capitalist paradigm. The publication of their post-independence creative writing raised political consciousness in countries where Blacks had always outnumbered whites by large percentages, but continued to suffer under the yoke of colonial traditions (i.e. segregation, racism, and genocide).[3]

In this chapter, I chose Marshall to begin the discussion on global political consciousness because of her complex multidimensional relationship to Black America and the Caribbean. As is evidenced in her essays and interviews which recall her upbringing within a West-Indian immigrant community in New York, Marshall's intellectual views transform the conceptualization of what it means to be a "Third World" activist/scholar. She has stated that her childhood memories are of an insular "Bajan" (Barbadian) community whose members refused what would be assumed or common connections between their experiences and the "shared" history of the American Black population. Therefore, though existing within similar confines of race and class in the urban north, both groups lived worlds apart.

Accordingly, the fictional heroines Marshall creates are typically caught between their national identity (e.g. American) and their Diasporic identities. They represent the intimate connection between western Africa and eastern America's shores, a connection which is littered with the bodies and souls of thousands of African people lost to the Middle Passage during the trans-Atlantic slave trade. Therefore, Marshall's novels often involve a Black American protagonist finding her own identity through a confrontation with symbols of an African past. Marshall's writing allows the reader to delve into both the complexities of loss associated with detachment from a universal Black community, as well as possibilities for change and renewal.

I consider Paule Marshall's Black revolutionary era novel, *The Chosen Place, The Timeless People* (1969), as another offering that can be read using the *Afro-Politico Womanist* framework because of its representation of an indigenous Caribbean community struggling to survive against the backdrop of post-colonialism. Like the other novels in this study, *The Chosen Place* has at its center a Black female activist whose interests rest in protecting the community from the outside, while working with the masses. The novel challenges the ideal of the Black elite "leading" the masses to a shared victory, and exposes how the colonial past, internal corruption, outside influence, and local hopelessness create a mélange of experiences that are not specific to the Caribbean region. Marshall connects the histories of white Jewish, African American, Black and white Caribbean people to comment on the universality of longing and loss associated with physical and psychic displacement.

The setting of *The Chosen Place* is the fictional Bourne Island, where indigenous Blacks have become separated according to caste, ideology, and class. Those who live in "Bournehills," the older underdeveloped portion of the island represent the poor and working classes. The physical infrastructure of the Bournehills has suffered due to a dearth of economic support as well as a resistance to the outside influence of foreign investors. Marshall repeatedly describes the main road in the lower section that disappears after a heavy rain. It is "washed-out" and impassable, yet eventually rebuilt by local men. Like Sisyphus, the indigenous community seems (at least from the outside) doomed to the never ending cycle of progress and decline.

On the opposite side of Bourne Island life middle-class islanders and foreign dignitaries function and reside in other, more developed sections of the island. These men and their wives inhabit colonial mansions and similar edifices which are a constant reminder of the island's past. They have come back "home" from being educated in British universities abroad where they exported their culture and reinforced British customs. They are described as follows:

> . . . nearly all the men there were senior civil servants and high-ranking government officials. The rest were members of the professions, which in Bourne Island were largely taken to mean only medicine and law . . . They were all, to a man almost, drinking imported whisky, scorning as a matter of status the local rum . . . all wearing dark-toned, conservative, heavy English suits in spite of the hot night . . . Some [like the permanent secretary] had on matching vests, and a few wore their old school ties (Marshall 53).

Within their respective offices, the men described above control the economic future of Bourne Island. Island industry is a throwback to one hundred years of British rule and colonization, when Bourne Island was a major contributor to the sugar industry. Likewise, sugarcane remains cultivated by Bournehills residents and the island's economic stability rests on foreign investors, tourism, and humanitarian projects. The influx of "outsiders" has created animosity among local communities—with the Bournehills residents subversively rejecting the commodification of their culture through tourism.

Throughout the novel, various acts of resistance by the residents actively prevent the silencing of the indigenous voice discussed at the beginning of this chapter, but do not always affect corruption within the government. Significantly, the text depicts the agency indigenous communities have in deciding their own progress. In tandem with this power is the responsibility of Black women to preserve the history and culture of the community through education and historical narrative.

Marshall introduces the individual lives and stories of Bournehills people through the voice of Merle Kinbona, a woman who becomes the representative of the "folk." She enters the novel with a cool confidence that belies her fierceness and complexity. Much attention is given (by the author) to her attire and accessories—all outward statements of her politics and experiences. She is described wearing the following:

> . . . a flared print dress made from cloth of a vivid abstract tribal motif: cloth from the sun, from another cosmos, which could have been found draped in offhand grace around a West African market woman. Pendant silver earrings carved in the form of those saints to be found on certain European churches . . . Numerous bracelets, also of silver . . . But these, unlike the earrings, were heavy, crudely made, and noisy (Marshall 4–5).

Merle exists as the consummate Diasporic subject wearing clothing, jewelry, and shoes that speak to her intercultural subjectivity. She is from Bourne Island, has studied in England, been to Africa, and stopped along other ports of the Middle Passage, all the while calling for a "revolution."

Like Merle's surname suggests, she represents the "family goods" of a community that is unable and often unwilling to speak for themselves. Her origins are in Bournehills, though she has traveled and lived abroad for a number of years. Merle, like few others, chose to return to her *native land*[4] in an effort to save herself and "the Little Fella," (the masses). Her personal experiences abroad haunt her and she frequently has "breakdowns" and periodically secludes herself from others (117). Deemed a champion of the community, she is the listening ear and political voice of those around her and is described as single-handedly representing "the entire spurned and shameless lot" (67).

As a former teacher and activist she has often been dismissed from Bourne-Island politics because of insubordinate acts, like teaching an unedited history of the island to her students or celebrating the memory of slave revolutions during the colonial period. Merle's emphasis on ground-level insurgency counters what Caribbean-born writers like Michelle Cliff call a "primary colonial identification" with England and America (Cliff 17). Through the process of turning the critical gaze inward Merle attempts to decolonize the minds of her students and calls attention to the impact colonization has on the island's inhabitants. She posits facts such as, "Those English were the biggest obeah men out when you considered what they did to our minds." She later echoes Marx in her proclamation that "The church and the rumshop . . . [are] one and the same, you know. Both a damn conspiracy to keep us pacified and in ignorance. Just you wait, though, come the revolution we're going to ban them both! (Marshall 133)

Merle's attitudes and activist practices (speaking up for the masses, campaigning for their right to "fete" as they wish, and educating those around her) reflect the tenets of cognitive liberation, or "the set of circumstances most likely to facilitate the transformation from hopeless submission to oppressive conditions to an aroused readiness to challenge those conditions" (McAdam 34). She understands the collective power associated with accepting and appreciating Black national culture. In *The Wretched of the Earth* Frantz Fanon states:

> The claim to a national culture in the past does not only rehabilitate that nation and serve as a justification for the hope of a future national culture. In the sphere of psycho-affective equilibrium it is responsible for an important change in the native . . . By a kind of perverted

logic, [Colonialism] turns the past of the oppressed people, and distorts, disfigures, and destroys it (Fanon 210).

Obviously, while the awareness of ones' political situation does not *guarantee* active political participation, exposure to inequalities in the political process is a significant precursor to insurgent action.

As seen in *Meridian* with Truman Held's accomodationist ideals and the references in *Song of Solomon* to the selfish and cold-hearted Macon Dead, the Black elite on the island has also severed their social bond with the masses. In their eyes, the people in the poor community are unworthy of the "special" treatment and external resources funneled into the community by external corporations. For example, the current topic on the island are the white American delegates (Saul, his wife Harriet, and Allen) from the Center for Applied Social Research (CASR), an organization interested in "helping" the poor in Bournehills progress socially and economically. The Black elite are opposed to CASR's presence because they consider any effort place on the betterment of Bournehills to be a wasted one. The argument is that many groups have come in the past and have failed at their mission because the masses do not want to help themselves.

At the welcome reception for Saul and the rest of the CASR crew, the upper crust of the island warn the visitors against "those people" in "the hills." The prominent "Black men" who "call[ed] to mind some slightly outmoded, upper-class Victorian gentlemen of the turn of the century," castigate the masses for their non-progressive attitudes toward building a better future. One attendee explains:

> . . . You don't know that place. There's no changing or improving it. You people could set up a hundred development schemes at a hundred million each and down there would remain the same . . . [T]he small farmers' co-operative government tried starting there a few years back . . . nearly caused a war down there . . . Work their crops together? Share with each other? Not those people. The poor co-operative officer had to run for his life (56).

And later,

> . . . I tell you, Bournehills is someplace out of the Dark Ages . . . And the television set that British firm gave them for the social center played one day and then mysteriously broke down . . . the jukebox from America didn't last a week . . . There's no understanding those people, I tell you!

Saul ignores their negative attitudes and condescending manner toward those "beneath" them and later acknowledges, "God, the middle class is the same the world over" (74). What is important to note is the faulty logic used to "understand" the actions of "those people." In a show of solidarity, the men at the reception attempt to warn Saul against a significant economic loss if he places too much emphasis on restructuring the Bournehills community. What is lost in this exchange is the reason for the repeated rejection of foreign aid, methods of crop production, and/or entertainment. For the residents of Bournehills to completely benefit from any external resources, they understand that the needs of the community must be defined internally. Including the emphasis on co-operative crop production, the items mentioned above are speculative desires and do not speak to the wishes of the people. In "Urban Social Movements, 'Race' and Community," Paul Gilroy provides an analysis of "the political and cultural vitality" of Black British social movements. In the essay he writes of the disparity between the larger community and the goals of the leaders. He explains,

> Community is as much about difference as it is similarity and identity.
> It is a relational idea which suggests . . . the idea of antagonism—
> domination and subordination between one community and another.
> The word directs analysis to the boundary between these groups. It
> is a boundary which is presented primarily by symbolic means and
> therefore a broad range of meanings can co-exist around it reconciling
> individuality and commonality and competing definitions of what the
> movement is about. The political rhetoric of leaders is, after all, not a
> complete guide to the motivations and aspirations of those who play a
> less prominent role (Gilroy 415).

Though written within a Black British context, Gilroy's analysis of community and the existence of "competing definitions" for political action fit into most examinations of internally defined movement goals. What the island leaders fail to realize is that the stubborn resistance of the Bournehills residents is representative of a cultural history of survival and liberation on their own terms.

The islanders hold on to the resilience of their forefather "Cuffee Ned" who led the only successful slave revolt on the island, and burned the crops with a fire that lasted "five days," (a contested number that provides scenes of comic relief in the novel). It was not until the British planters captured 'Ned' and placed his head on a stake for all the islanders to see, that they were able to subdue the revolutionaries' actions. But as one hears in the oft-told history throughout the text, the significance of the revolt is what drives the islanders. They find comfort in knowing that one of their own took control over his own destiny in an attempt to lead his people to freedom. Therefore, today the Bournehills residents exist as a nation within a nation defining their own lives.

By refusing aid/gifts from England and America, they prevent the possibility of external government rule by those neo-colonizing nations that seek to conquer and control what was once theirs. Though the Black leaders on the island disagree with Bournehills methods and consider the community "lost" and ignorant, as Gilroy explains above, the "motivations and aspirations" of the masses are not readily understood by (or even aligned with) a leadership base that remains separate from the community. For Bournehills, to rise, the people must define their terms. Likewise, it is not until the end of the novel that even Saul can understand the lessons the people in Bournehills are trying to teach those who infiltrate from the outside. In a conversation with Merle, he thinks about how programs like the one funded by CASR can be more effective. He states, "I'm more than ever convinced now that that's the best way: to have people from the country itself carry out their own development programs whenever possible. Outsiders just complicate the picture" (Marshall 467).

Shortly before Saul leaves the island and Merle moves to reconcile with her estranged family in Africa, the people begin to organize. Through cooperative efforts, the research team is successful in getting the residents interested in a citizen's council that could be instrumental in addressing grievances. Also, the council would enable the residents to elect representatives who could truly "speak" on behalf of the Bournehills district. This success should not be read as solely attributed to Saul's presence on the island, or Merle's encouragement, though both factors are important. Like the sweeper who speaks to Truman in the first scene of Meridian, Bournehills has "seen rights come and has seen 'em go," but in the end, they are left with the reassurance that they can realize their dreams of economic and political freedom through their own efforts—without a leader-focused agenda. Although Merle claims she is "waiting on a messiah . . . a tough somebody this time," to rescue the community, she knows the people will survive whether or not they perform according to outwardly-defined notions of "progress." As a people, they maintain self-sufficiency.

While Marshall fictionalizes political and economic challenges that many island nations faced post-independence, later non-fiction works like Jamaica Kincaid's *A Small Place*, for example, also speak to the prevalence of nepotism and greed in these contexts. In a poignant look at the political situation present in her native island of Antigua, Jamaica Kincaid manages to capture all aspects of the island as well as implicate the reader in the destruction of the island's values. *A Small Place* displays the intense frustration of a native Antiguan as she surveys the corrupt government and stifling dependence on external resources that lies beneath the façade of a beautiful island. She manipulates the gaze that is normally associated with the colonizer and forces the reader/tourist to see the truth behind the scenic view. The text is divided into four parts that tell the story of a present and past riddled with phases of colonization, slavery, tourism, and poverty.

Kincaid begins the text with an unforgiving view of tourism and its problems. She reminds the reader, "since (you) are a tourist, the thought of what it might be like for someone who had to live day in, day out in a place that suffers constantly from drought, and so has to watch carefully every drop of fresh water used . . . must never cross your mind (Kincaid 4). She continues throughout the text to criticize all aspects of tourism and shows the reader how the island's culture suffers because of outside "visitors." Kincaid also ridicules Antiguan politics and argues that the inhabitants of the island remain in a state of mental slavery. Economics, the distribution of power, and governmental alliances are also addressed throughout the text.

Like Bourne Island, most of the island's economic resources come from the "outside." The philosophy of "decision-making power (being) concentrated in the hands of the few as opposed to the many" is a reality for the non-influential inhabitants of most island nations (Greenberg 5). The ministers of government who control the island's commerce represent the "few." When assessing the economic disparities in Antigua, Kincaid observes that "all the cars you see are brand-new, or almost brand-new, and that they are all Japanese-made" (Kincaid 6). These cars are "very expensive" and do not compare to the quality of life afforded to the indigenous people. Kincaid notes that,

> . . . the person driving this brand-new car filled with the wrong gas lives in a house that, in comparison, is far beneath the status of the car; and if you were to ask why you would be told that the banks are encouraged by the government to make loans available for cars, but loans for houses not so easily available; and if you ask again why, you will be told that the two main car dealerships in Antigua are owned in part or outright by ministers in government (Kincaid 7).

Deals made with external investors benefit the elite of the Antiguan society and are not used to improve the conditions of the island's economy. In his assessment on Antigua and its economic situation, Mark Kurlansky writes, "Foreign investors are offered a dream tax code with no income tax and a ten-to-fifteen-year holiday on business taxes. This has meant that the country lacks a tax base and had little in the treasury for non-tourist-related services" (Kurlansky 24). This translates to a nearly non-existent monetary fund and a direct reliance upon "foreign investors."

What is significant about all of the works and references included in this chapter is the emphasis on the complicity of global Black middle class in the continued destruction of the global Black community. While the dilemma is not novel and/or unique to one region or country (as evidenced in this project), nevertheless, what authors like Marshall demonstrate through their literary critique of unsupported grass-roots activism, is the fact that the success of slavery, colonization and domination is the dissolution of a self-supporting community structure with the needs of the collective at the center.

Conclusion

"We are the last generation who remember the power of viable Black communities. We were raised near or by grandparents who did not buy into desegregation and the quest for wealth, because they couldn't. They were from another time. Ironically, it was for them that our parents fought against the system, and later it was for us. But who are we fighting for? We need to wake up and realize that those that come after us do not have the privilege of our ancestral knowledge. Why are we content to let them wander in the dark?"

—KE

In the end, the fictional works examined in this project include representations of Black women who make conscious choices to speak within and about the current challenges of the Black community during the post-Civil Rights period. The initial decision made by the authors reflects their own understanding of a Womanist-based political agenda that involves an entire population on the verge of a spiritual breakdown. Through the medium of fiction, the writers prove that the role of the Black female activist is not to be the sole voice of her family, community, and race, but to be one of many voices of progress and change. Throughout this project the focus has been on the ways Black women writers reflected political discourse of the Post-Civil Rights era in their fiction. By examining and understanding their original statements we are able to cast a reflective glance on the messages within specific texts.

As seen in Marshall's *The Chosen Place, The Timeless People* , a community can only progress once the members begin to imagine the possibility of a different, better space. The choice of the Bournehills residents to remain retrospective has its place within the context of struggle. The Adinkra symbol "Sankofa," which means one does not know where he is going unless he knows where he has been rings true within the context of Black insurgency, and collective remembrance of struggle and dispossession often serves as the basis for current collective action. Cuffee Ned and his fearless revolt is the Sankofa symbol for the Bournehills residents. Likewise *The Chosen Place* shows us how, as Frantz Fanon posits, the "weakness" of the oppressed is not only the result of colonialism, but also "the result of the intellectual laziness of the national middle class, of its spiritual penury, and of the profoundly cosmopolitan mold that its mind is set in" (Fanon 149).

Likewise, *The Salt Eaters* as a narrative of hope regained is also able to critique failures and applaud success. In the novel, the survival of the community depends on Velma's decision to continue fighting for everyone around her, including herself. In opposition to the model of a solitary female protagonist working within the community, Toni Cade Bambara places Minnie Ransom and Velma together. They feed off each other, as one needs the other in order to survive. Symbolically, Minnie as an elder cannot let Velma go because as a member of the younger generation Velma holds the key to Claybourne's survival. Through her confused dream state, Velma realizes that it is Minnie's traditional healing practices keeping her alive.

Thus, the old and the young within the community must work together to combat the external evil that seeks to destroy progressive action. This realization is significant when thinking about the tenuous connections between cultural and revolutionary nationalism and the ideologies upon which they are based. Cultural nationalism is steeped in the concept of a return to ancestral traditions and the recognition of African retentions (i.e. the "old"), and Revolutionary nationalism embraces a coming revolution fueled by the collective force of people of color worldwide (i.e. the "new"). The underlying argument of *The Salt Eaters* and the lesson to be learned as a result of the rift between nationalisms is: one cannot survive without the other.

A similar lesson is learned in *Song of Solomon*. Though probably the least utopian of the three novels, there is encouragement in the fact that Milkman Dead comes alive after connecting with his past in the form of his aunt Pilate and the eventual quest on which he embarks. The lessons he learns resulting from his obsession with retrospectives affect how he handles present realities and his goals for the future. Like Velma, Milkman and Pilate face a community on the brink of an uncertain future. Though the community is isolated from the rest of the world, the damaging effects of hopelessness, poverty, and despair fill the streets and produce a restless tension. Instead of channeling the energy toward community empowerment and change, both Guitar and Milkman, as representations of revolutionary and cultural nationalism, choose to fight against each other for the same wealth. Guitar wants to kill Milkman over allegedly stolen "gold" and

Milkman in turn wants Guitar's life because he threatens his own and the lives of those around him—his gold. Thus, the war continues and in the end each man leaps forward to a probable death. Only the acknowledgement of Pilate's wisdom can save either of them, as she represents the survival of the Black community.

In *Meridian* the title character does not differentiate between past and present. Time stands still as Walker merges events in Meridian's life to demonstrate how Black political history is not separate from current struggles—only interwoven. Meridian's willingness to see the plight of the people around her as existing on a continuum of political and social responsibility, places her at odds with the rest of the world, but at peace with herself. The community's future rests in her continued activism and the return of those who escaped the oppression of Southern racism and injustice. For Meridian, she cannot move on until her former brothers and sisters in the struggle understand that their place is with those masses left behind in a mad dash to reach the elusive finish line.

Each of the examined communities harbor some form of chaos and/or disillusionment that prevents it from moving forward. Whether it is the psychological damage done to the inhabitants of a postcolonial island nation, the fear and poverty that exists within the small southern communities that Meridian "visits," the postmodern fragmentation that permeates the neighborhoods in Bambara's Claybourne, Georgia, or the secluded and indifferent community of Virginia that holds the key to Milkman's past, present, and future—the challenges are plentiful. As a result of the social climate in the small towns, the protagonists function as repositories of possible solutions to the problems facing dying communities in the post-Civil Rights era.

As texts that can be read under the Afro-Politico Womanism paradigm, *Song of Solomon*, *Meridian*, *The Salt Eaters*, and *The Chosen Place, The Timeless People* contain pointed critiques of class structures, organizational leadership, and the absence of collective action within the Black community. The characters analyzed above, as well as the communities in which they reside represent a larger connection to the political history of Black resistance. This project suggests the endless possibilities for change once the community as a cohesive unit is prepared and willing to address the needs of the collective. While the aims of this hopeful reasoning may appear idealistic and unrealistic, Afro-Politico Womanism as a way of understanding the needs within the community provides space to use an alternate lens when defining the failures and successes of the Civil Rights and immediate post-Civil Rights era. Through close readings of the novels offered in this study, one can see the revolutionary dreams of the authors as progressive visions for the future.

Though the focus of the literary analyses in this project were novels written by Black women, it is possible to read comparable Black revolutionary era fiction written by Black men through the same lens. Examples include John Edgar Wideman's *The Lynchers* (1973) in which "the masses" are depicted as lost and uncertain, like those in *The Salt Eaters*. Significantly, the protagonist of the novel is a middle class Black man who has decided to return to the poor and working class community in an effort to further political mobilization. Other offerings include Sam Greenlee's earlier novel, *The Spook Who Sat By the Door* (1969). This novel also critiques the return of the Black middle class to a struggling and ignored Black community, this time in a radical attempt at political mobilization.

As stated throughout this project, APW represents several aims for understanding the methods by which activists (recognized and unrecognized) conduct practical "work" within the post-Civil Rights Black community. "Community" is used to define the general body of Black citizens who have historically been excluded from reaping social "gains" from the Movement. Traditionally, the masses (as they are often deemed) are left out of the decision-making processes and are unable to attain the political power necessary to advance their collective situations due to the failures of leadership. As a community-based approach, the concept works within pre-existing internal structures, eliminating a focus on issues external to the needs of a multidimensional community. This emphasis on available internal resources seeks to eliminate the usurpation of power by those deemed more "qualified." The model assumes an understanding of various culturally and racially specific experiences and personal histories that comprise the whole. As a theoretical approach, APW provides options for understanding the genre of revolutionary narratives and literatures of the Black Aesthetic.

As was necessary during the Civil Rights and Black Revolutionary period that followed, the definition of goals by the masses must remain at the heart of an active social and political global agenda. The question remains: who is the true voice of the subaltern if it is not herself? In the introduction to *Moving Beyond Boundaries: Volume I,* Carole Boyce Davies speaks to the public perception of silence that marks Black women caught within a paradoxical space of the heard and unheard. She writes,

> I begin by asserting that it is not only the condition of silence and voicelessness that seems the most pressing at this historical moment but the function of *hearing* or *listening* on the part of those who wield oppressive power. . . . The appropriate critique of the inability of oppressors to HEAR allows for more resistance. . . . [M]any black women have

spoken incessantly without fully being heard and have often reached the point where they say nothing verbally and instead operate from a silence which often speaks eloquently (Davies 3).

I include this quote because the authors examined within this project fall under the category of "speaking without fully being heard" within the context of political discourse and social commentary. Although their writing reflects a deep understanding of the problems that plagued oppressed and depressed people, the message of hope, rebuilding, and self-love is absent when an assessment of influential doctrine is noted. During a presentation in 1981, Molara Ogundipe-Leslie speaks to the overlooked power of critical social fiction when she observes that "seldom are calls made for the use of imaginative literature as a data source for the study of women and society" (Ogundipe-Leslie 43).

In large part, the context of this project rests with destroyed post-Civil Rights idealism and the lasting legacy affecting the current state of Black America. In all the novels, there is a slight sense of loss associated with the community and individual women's lives. This act of foreboding works as an omen of disappearing Black activism—a desire to remain invested in saving Black lives through the connection to the community, even after everyone else has gone home. The female activists who support the *Afro-Politico Womanist* agenda "step up" to the task at hand while the appointed leadership is away debating the next course of action. Overall, the novels in this study end with a question mark for the future. At the end of twenty-six years of national political unrest, no one knew what the future held for the Black community. The community was truly at a crossroads.

In the immediate decade following this study (1980), Black communities across the nation were thrown into utter chaos resulting from misguided conservative agendas and internal division. During the tumultuous 1980s, (or the Reagan-era) a stark rise in crime, violence, death, drug use, and poverty plagued urban Black communities. Federal legislative debates over the fate of the "welfare queen" and the "crack addict" did little to actively address genocide within inner-city neighborhoods—especially since the misnomers were racialized and gendered in an attempt to further demonize the minority communities. Also, during this period, aside from (or rather as a result of) white conservative backlash, members of the Black middle class turned an otherwise paternalistic eye away from poor and working class communities and placed their hope in a new day.

The affects of abandonment on the masses were further disillusionment, desperation, and despair. In a much earlier time, the community had seen this before. The late 19th century through the turn of the 20th century ushered in the "New Negro" who represented educated elite, severely distant from the Black proletariat he represented in the national arena. During this time Black female scholars like Anna Julia Cooper warned her audience of the dangers associated with ignoring the masses. In *A Voice From the South* she instructs:

> "Not by pointing to sun-bathed mountain tops do we prove that Phoebus warms the valleys. We must point to homes, average homes, homes of the rank and file of horny handed toiling men and women of the South (where the masses are) lighted and cheered by the good, the beautiful, and the true,—then and not till then will the whole plateau be lifted into the sunlight (Cooper 30–31).

Many women throughout the 20th century, like Cooper, understood that "the masses" set the pulse of racial progress and their viability is the strength of those they help support. But unfortunately, the roster is also filled with the names of prominent figures and leaders who fought alongside the members of the community, only to leave them behind when the destination appeared near. Whereas before, the Black community was largely intertwined and internally supported, the "new day" brought external leadership, realignment of political loyalties, and a resurgent Black intelligentsia focused on assessing from the outside, rather than working from within.

I end with the following sentiments made by Merle Kinbona in *The Chosen Place, The Timeless People* about her present condition. The statements are significant because they aptly mirror the ongoing dilemmas facing the Black community. She states,

> 'I am like someone bewitched, turned foolish. It's like my very will's gone. And nothing short of a miracle will bring it back I know. Something has to happen—I don't know what, but something—and apart from me (because it's out of my hands I'm convinced) to bring me back to myself. *Something that's been up has to come down . . .* before I can get moving again!' (Marshall 230) (Emphasis mine).

Notes

NOTES TO CHAPTER ONE

1. In this project I frequently use the term "community" as representative of the Black masses. This includes poor and working class, rural and urban Blacks who are connected via a common cultural heritage that speaks to a shared history of slavery, subjugation, oppression, economic depression, organization, the affirmation of racial pride, and shared political goals.

2. In 1974, Alice Walker defined Womanism as: "From *womanish*. (Opp. Of girlish, frivolous, irresponsible, not serious) A black feminist or feminist of color. From the black folk expression of mothers to female children, "You acting womanish," i.e. like a woman. Usually referring to outrageous, audacious, courageous, or willful behavior . . . Appreciates and prefers women's culture, women's emotional flexibility (values tears as natural counter-balance of laughter), and women's strength . . . Committed to survival and wholeness of entire people, male and female. Not a separatist, except for health. Traditionally universalist . . . Loves struggle. Loves the Folk. Loves herself. Regardless" (Excerpt)

3. Noninstitutionalized tactics "represent . . . a distinct challenge to elite groups. [The tactics] communicate a fundamental rejection of the established institutional mechanisms for seeking redress of group grievances; substantively, it deprives elite groups of their recourse to institutional power" (McAdam 57).

4. Though I focus primarily on four well-known authors who have written texts that fit under the Afro-Politico Womanist paradigm, I am aware of several other contemporary authors and novels produced during the time period specified that speak to the plight of the Black community. For example, Gloria Naylor's *The Women of Brewster Place*; Carlene Polite's *The Flagellants*, and *Sister X and the Victims of Foul Play*; Alice Walker's *In Love and Trouble* and *The Third Life of Grange Copeland*, Paule Marshall's *Praisesong for the Widow*. Also included on this list are other writers like, Margaret Walker, Octavia Butler, and Gayl Jones.

5. The term "real revolution" is derived from Alice Walker's observations that "the real revolution is always concerned with the least glamorous stuff." Like teaching children to read, registering disenfranchised Blacks to vote, preserving history, etc.

NOTES TO CHAPTER TWO

1. All references to "Black Nationalism" are in the American context, unless otherwise noted.

2. The types of Black Nationalism listed are taken from Van Deburg's *New Day in Babylon* (1992) and Dean Robinson's *Black Nationalism in American Politics and Thought* (2001).

3. I am identifying the first three waves of American Black revolution as: Slave rebellions, Black political participation during Southern Reconstruction, and the formation of Black nationalist organizations during the early years of the 20th century.

4. I take this term from Dean Robinson's *Black Nationalism in American Politics and Thought* (2001).

5. In this chapter I argue that Revolutionary Nationalism and Cultural Nationalism as represented by specific organization within the Black Power movement were placed in opposition to one another. Despite the controversial rhetorical and ideological battles waged over the terms, both types of nationalism have several important similarities. For example, the primary goal of both ideologies was to ensure a national identity that would place the Black American on an even par with his American compatriots. This includes but is not limited to: an emphasis on mental and physical liberation, economic stability, social and racial justice, an end to discriminatory practices, and unity within the Black community.

6. Although, the debate over the inclusion of "white liberals in the struggle" became a hot point and caused a rift in many revolutionary organizations, such as the Student Non-Violent Coordinating Committee (SNCC) and the Black Panther Party for Self-Defense.

7. Throughout this chapter, I will use the terms "Black Revolutionary Movement" and "Black Power Movement" interchangeably.

8. Stewart, Maria. "On African Rights and Liberty" (1833), in *Civil Rights Since 1787: A Reader on the Struggle.* Eds. Jonathan Birnbaum and Clarence Taylor.

9. The term accomodationist is widely used. I am using the definition used in Bush's *We Are Not What We Seem* (1999).

10. Though Robert F. Williams did not consider the terms "nationalist" or "revolutionary nationalist" useful or relevant, his seminal text *Negroes with Guns* was widely read and served as a reference for the ideological basis of the revolutionary nationalist standpoint.

11. This statement is similar to Maulana Karenga's argument that "nationalism is a precondition for revolution, it is culture that is the primary vehicle

for achieving this national awareness and commitment" qtd. in Flowers'
Pens of Fire (1996).

12. The mythic tale of African slaves from the Igbo tribe who were brought in
chains to the "Gullah" or Low Country islands off the coast of Georgia
and South Carolina. Legend has it that after surveying the "situation" the
slaves turned back to the ocean and flew back "home" to Africa, one by
one. There are several literary and oral presentations of the mythic "Flying Africans." See *The People Who Could Fly*, *Praisesong for the Widow*,
Daughters of the Dust, among other transcribed folktales from former
slaves like "All God's Chillun Got Wings," for example.

13. Psalms 68:31

14. Historian Robin D.G. Kelley's *Freedom Dreams* (2002) provides a comprehensive analysis of the impact Marcus Garvey's movement had on the
Black community of the early 20th century.

15. In addition to Cruse, see Dean Robinson's *Black Nationalism in American
Politics and Thought*, as an example.

16. Comprehensive studies of these two organizations include *Fighting for US*
(2003) by Scot Brown, Philip Foner's *The Black Panthers Speak* (1970),
and sections in Van Deburg's *New Day in Babylon* (1992), and *We are not
what we seem* (1999) by Rod Bush.

17. Many scholars have noted the FBI's involvement in the dissolution of both
the US organization and the Black Panther Party for Self-Defense. FBI
records prove that informants were placed in specifically targeted Black
"radical" organizations as part of COINTELPRO (Counterintelligence Program) whose aim was to dissemble and dismantle militant organizations.
One tactic often used was instigation by the informants and the creation of
false rumors that would ensure tension between militant groups—allowing
them to destroy each other, naturally. See *Fighting for US* (2003) by Scot
Brown and *We are not what we seem* (1999) by Rod Bush for more discussions on this topic and the relationship between US and the Black Panther
Party for Self-Defense.

18. It is important to note that many of the Black revolutionary nationalists
referred to themselves as socialists at various junctures in the Black Power
movement.

19. See footnote 12.

NOTES TO CHAPTER THREE

1. Later we find that Truman does not march anymore because 'what [he]
believe[s] cannot be placed on a placard" (108).

2. A parody of Spelman College in Atlanta, Georgia. Spelman is an all female,
historically Black university.

3. In *Soul on Ice* (1968), Eldridge Cleaver admits that his motivation for rap-
ing white (and Black) women is to seek revenge on white men. For Cleaver,
violent sex with white women is about power and control.

4. Ironically, the university Truman attends (R. Baron College) is a reference to John D. Rockefeller, the "philanthropist" and robber baron who donated the current site of Morehouse College in Atlanta, Georgia. Morehouse, like the fictional R. Baron College, is an all male, historically Black university.

5. Many scholars have focused on the objectification of Marilene O'Shay in *Meridian* as it relates to Meridian's own position and silencing as a woman. For example, Lynn Pifer writes of the "issues" with presenting a mummified woman strangled because of her infidelity and inability to ascribe to the virtues of True Womanhood in her article "Coming to Voice in Alice Walker's *Meridian.*

6. Guano is composed of bat feces and was/is a common fertilizer in agricultural areas of the south. The children work in the plant preparing guano for distribution. It is important to note that in Toni Cade Bambara's *The Salt Eaters* there is also a reference to this type of work, as one of the characters laments the smell of "bat shit.'

7. The practice of preparing African-American students for society by neglecting to emphasize Black experience still exists at some Historically Black Colleges and Universities (HBCUs) today. I have had numerous conversations with alumni from various HBCUs who admit to not knowing "much" about Black history and/or not having the option to take classes like African American Literature because they were not offered in the curriculum. Many HBCUs do not provide students the option to major in Black or Diaspora Studies, whereas the majority of these programs are on the campuses of predominately white institutions.

NOTES TO CHAPTER FOUR

1. "Silent women" is a term that I contend within the larger project because of its reliance upon a belief that Black women who stepped aside and were often pushed back from the forefront of activist organizations were actually silent. I argue that omission and dismissal does not equate to silence. Though contemporary women have admitted to a conscious decision to fall back and let male leaders stand at the helm of the Black community, many others acknowledged the "necessity of egalitarian roles." See Pratibha Parmar's documentary "A place of Rage" and *"Together" Black Women* (1972) a sociological study by Inez Smith Reid, for commentary.

2. Although this reference and others in the chapter pre-date contemporary scholarship on Black womanhood and feminism, I include it because the issues it uncovers is immediately relevant to the publication date of the novel.

3. AFDC, American Families with Dependent Children program, originally called ADC (Aid to Dependent Children), more commonly known as "welfare."

4. The Lowndes County Freedom Party was an all-black political party in Alabama (1966). Called "SNCC's 1ˢᵗ experiment in exclusively Black activism," the party was responsible for political mobilization and voter

registration in a county where no Blacks were registered to vote. They used the symbol of the Black Panther, which was later adopted by the Black Panther Party for Self-Defense in Oakland, CA. For more information see Jonathan Foster's "Radical Loss: The First Black Panthers and the Lowndes County Election of 1966" *The Urban Historical Review* 5 (Spring 2001).

NOTES TO CHAPTER FIVE

1. Juliana Makuchi Nfah-Abbenyi recounts the issues raised by Gloria Hull surrounding the issue of "hegemonic and totalizing conceptualizations . . . by Anglo-American feminists" at the "Black Woman Writer and the Diaspora" conference in 1985. See *Gender in African Women's Writing* by Nfah-Abbenyi.

2. Examples include Binyavanga Wainaina's "How to write about Africa," Stuart Hodkinson's "How Rock Stars Betrayed the Poor," and critical backlash against the "I am African," campaign supported by former supermodel and human rights activist Iman. The ad campaign includes pictures of celebrities adorned with "war paint" with the caption "I am African" beneath their pictures. The premise is the fact that since the human genome project has been able to trace all human ancestry to Africa, every person is "African" and should be concerned about the AIDS ravaged continent.

3. Many of the Diasporic writers listed in this chapter were published after the chronological frame of this study, due to the increased opportunities for women to speak out publicly post-independence. As the evidence in this chapter argues, the authors were active and vocal before this time, but were "unheard."

4. This phrase is taken from the title of Aime Cesaire's groundbreaking work, *Notebook of a Return to My Native Land*, in which he offers the internal suffering of an assimilated islander living abroad, who longs to return to his native post-colonial island home.

Glossary

Afro-Poltico Womanist Agenda: a method for understanding how fiction by Black women writers provides space to consider the merger of cultural and revolutionary nationalism as a prime element of the Black political process.

Black Cultural Nationalism: The belief that Black people will not survive and/or "win" the revolutionary war against white America if they (black people) do not first know and accept their African identities and connect to their ancestral roots. A "celebration of blackness." Also defined as "visual artists, writers, songwriters, (and musicians) using cultural forms as weapons in the struggle for liberation" (Van Deburg 9). Often ridiculed by Black revolutionary nationalism for an allegedly absent political agenda, and pacifist policies.

Black Panther Party for Self-Defense, or "Black Panthers": Revolutionary Nationalist organization founded by Huey Newton and Bobby Seale, in Oakland, California in response to police brutality and social injustice in the African American neighborhoods in Oakland. Infamous for the "storming" of the capital building in Sacramento, CA, when Ronald Reagan was governor, in response to a California judicial move to ban the right to bear arms in the state. The Black Panthers were major players in the Black Power Movement between 1965–1975.

Black Power: Term introduced to mainstream white America through Stokely Carmichael's declaration during a 1966 Civil Rights movement "March Against Fear" in Greenwood, Mississippi, "The only way we gonna stop them white men from whuppin' us is to take over. We been saying freedom for six years and we ain't got nothin.' What we gonna start saying now is Black Power!" (Van Deburg 32). Black Power as a demand of justice and political rights has been used frequently throughout the 20th

century, as a rallying cry for oppressed masses of Black people. In a country (America) where the benefits of power are reserved for white Americans, "Black Power" signified a demand for equality (economic, political, and social) and the destruction of the white power elite.

Black Revolutionary Nationalism: The more "militant" branch of Black Nationalism. Black revolutionary nationalism was an anti-capitalist movement based in the teachings of Malcolm X, Mao Tsetung, Karl Marx, Robert F. Williams, and Frantz Fanon, among others. Also viewed as a standpoint based on rhetoric, justice, and community organization. The prevailing belief among revolutionary nationalists was that the oppressed cannot be completely free until the entire "system" is overthrown (Van Deburg 153).

COINTELPRO: The FBI's Counter Intelligence Program, created by J. Edgar Hoover in the early 20th century to "watch" and monitor subversive organizations and individuals. Figured prominently in the deportation of Marcus Garvey, a black revolutionary leader of the 1930s. Later, COINTELPRO is regarded as the impetus for dissention among black nationalists groups (i.e. The Black Panthers, and US), and the intra-organizational conflicts that led to mistrust, sabotage, and eventually betrayal. Often, FBI "informants" disguised as group leaders were responsible for starting dangerous rumors that led to feuds.

Nationalism: The attribution of goals and cooperative empowerment of a collective group of individuals connected via race, ethnicity, or other significant common grouping.

People's Army (PA): A group of George Jackson supporters, or "Jackson forces." George Jackson was "a BPP field marshal, and celebrated prison author" that was "assassinated (in 1971) at San Quentin Prison (California), while allegedly trying to escape" (Bush 217).

US: Cultural Black Nationalist organization headed by Ron Everett (now known as Maulana Karenga). "US set out to construct as new black culture based upon selected African traditions, for the purpose of launching a cultural revolution among African Americans at large" (Brown). US members adopted "natural" hairstyles, the Kiswahili language, African names, and founded programs within South Central Los Angeles. US is the founding organization of Kwanzaa, the African American holiday celebration practiced worldwide.

Bibliography

Alvarez, Sonia E. Guest Lecture. The Ohio State University. 15 May 2003.

Arnold, Millard, Ed. *Steve Biko: Black Consciousness in South Africa*. New York: Random House, 1978.

Asante, Molefi Kente and Abdulai S. Vandi, Eds. *Contemporary Black Thought: Alternative Analyses in Social and Behavioral Science*. Beverly Hills: SAGE, 1980.

Bambara, Toni Cade. *The Salt Eaters*. New York: Vintage Books, 1980.

Beale, Frances. "Double Jeopardy: To Be Black and Female." *The Black Woman.* Ed. Toni Cade. New York: New American Library, 1970.

Bell, Derrick. *Faces at the Bottom of the Well: The Permanence of Racism*. New York: Basic Books, 1992.

Bethel, Lorraine and Barbara Smith. *The Black Women's Issue*. Brooklyn, N.Y. : Conditions, 1979.

Bhavnani, Kum-Kum. Editor. *Feminism and Race*. Oxford: Oxford University, 2001.

Billingslea-Brown, Alma. *Crossing Borders Through Folklore: African American Women's Fiction and Art*. Columbia: U of Missouri P, 1999.

Birnbaum, Jonathan and Clarence Taylor. *Civil Rights Since 1787: A Reader on the Struggle*. New York: New York UP, 2000.

Blair, Thomas. *Retreat to the Ghetto: The End of a Dream?* New York: Hill and Wang, 1977.

Blumberg, Rhoda Lois. "Women in the Civil Rights Movement: Reform or Revolution?" *Women and Revolution: Global expressions* Ed. M.J. Diamond Dordrecht. Boston: Kluwer Academic Publishers, 1998.

Bond, Jean Carey and Patricia Peery. "Is the Black Male Castrated?" in *The Black Woman: An Anthology*. Ed. Toni Cade. New York: New American Library, 1970. 141–148.

Brehon, Helen Cade. "Looking Back" *The Black Woman: An Anthology*. Ed. Toni Cade. New York: New American Library, 1970.

Brown, Scot. "The US Organization, Black Power Vanguard Politics, and the United Front Ideal: Los Angeles and Beyond" The Black Scholar 31:3–4. Fall-Winter 2001: 21–30.

Bush, Rod. *We are not what we seem: Black Nationalism and Class Struggle in the American Century.* New York: New York UP, 1999.

Cade, Toni, ed. *The Black Woman: An Anthology.* New York: New American Library, 1970.

Carby, Hazel. *Reconstructing Womanhood: The Emergence of the Afro-American Woman Novelist.* New York: Oxford UP, 1987.

Carmichael, Stokely, and Charles Hamilton. "The Black Power Revolt." *Black Power: the politics of liberation in America.* New York: Random House, 1967.

———. *Stokely Speaks: Black Power Back to Pan-Africanism.* New York: Random House, (1965) 1971.

Chapman, Tracy. "Talking 'Bout A Revolution." *Tracy Chapman.* Elektra, 1988.

Christian, Barbara. "'Somebody Forgot to Tell somebody something': African American Women's Historical Novels" in *Feminism and Race.* Kum-Kum Bhavnani, Editor. Oxford: Oxford University, 2001.

Clarke, John Henrik. "Reclaiming the Lost African Heritage." *Black Fire: An Anthology of Afro-American Writing.* Ed. Leroi Jones and Larry Neal. New York: William Morrow & Co. 1968.

Cliff, Michelle. "If I Could Write This in Fire I Would Write This in Fire" in *Home Girls: A Black Feminist Anthology.* Ed. Barbara Smith. New York: Kitchen Table Women of Color Press. 1983. 15–30.

Collins, Patricia Hill. "The Social Construction of Black Feminist Thought." *Feminism and Race.* Ed. Kum-Kum Bhavnani. New York : Oxford University Press, 2001.

———. *Fighting Words: Black Women and the Search for Justice.* Minneapolis: U of Minnesota P, 1998.

———. *Black Feminist Thought: Knowledge, Consciousness, and the Politics of Empowerment.* Second Edition. New York: Routledge. 2000.

Crass, Chris. "Beyond Welfare Queens: developing a race, class, and gender analysis of Welfare and Welfare Reform." *Colours of Resistance.* 3 Aug. 2004 <http://www.colours.mahost.org/articles/crass6.html>.

Cruse, Harold. "Revolutionary Nationalism and the Afro-American." Reprint. *Black Fire: An Anthology of Negro Writing.* Eds. Leroi Jones and Larry Neal. New York: William Morrow & Co. 1968. 39–63.

Davies, Carole Boyce. "Hearing Black Women's Voices: transgressing Imposed Boundaries." *Moving Beyond Boundaries Volume 1: International Dimensions of Black Women's Writing.* Eds. Carole Boyce Davies and 'M lara Ogundipe-Leslie. New York: NYU Press, 1995. 3–14.

———. *Moving Beyond Boundaries Volume 2: Black Women's Diasporas.* New York: NYU Press, 1995.

Davis, Angela. *Women, Culture and Politics.* New York: Vintage. 1990.

Davis, Joseph E., Ed. *Stories of Change: Narrative and Social Movement.* Albany: State
U of New York, 2002.

Davis, Kimberly Chabot. "Postmodern Blackness: Toni Morrison's *Beloved* and the end of history." *Twentieth Century Literature.* Summer (1998). New York: Hofstra UP. <http://www.findarticles.com/p/articles/mi_m0403/is_2_44/ai_53260178/pg_ 1.>

Dubey, Madhu. *Black Women Novelists and the National Aesthetic.* Bloomington : Indiana UP, 1994.

Du Bois, W.E.B. *The Souls of Black Folk.* New York: Blue Heron, 1953. New York: Modern Library, 1996.

Eagleton, Terry. *The Illusions of Postmodernism.* Cambridge: Blackwell Publishers, 1996.

Elia, Nada *Trances, Dances, and Vociferations: Agency and Resistance in Africana Women's Narratives.* New York: Garland, 2001. 151.

"Eyes on the Prize: Power!" WGBH Boston, a production of Blackside, Inc. Jon Else, Series Producer; Judy Richardson, Series Associate Producer, Steve Fayer, Series Writer. Atlanta: Turner Home Entertainment; Alexandria: PBS Home Video, 1995.

Fanon, Frantz. *The Wretched of the Earth.* New York: Grove, 1963.

Fatton, Robert. *Black Consciousness in South Africa.* Albany: State University of New York, 1986.

Fleming, Cynthia Griggs. "Black Women and Black Power: The Case of Ruby Doris Smith Robinson and the Student Nonviolent Coordinating Committee." *Sisters in the Struggle: African American Women in the Civil Rights-Black Power Movement.* Ed. Bettye Collier-Thomas and V.P. Franklin. New York: New York U P, 2001.

Flowers, Sandra Hollin. *African American Nationalist Literature of the 1960s: Pens of Fire.* New York: Garland Publishing, 1996.

Foner, Philip S. *The Black Panthers Speak.* Philadelphia: J.B. Lippincott, 1970.

Gates, Henry Louis. *The Signifyin' Monkey: A Theory of Afro-American Literary Criticism.* New York: Oxford UP, 1988.

Gilyard, Keith. "The Social Responsibility that Writing Is—And writing Instruction, too." *Writing Lives: Reading Communities.* Eds. Kay Halasek, Edgar Singleton, et al. 2000.

Gilroy, Paul. "Urban Social Movements, 'Race' and Community." *Colonial Discourse and Post-Colonial Theory: A Reader.* Eds. Patrick Williams and Laura Chrisman. New York: Columbia University, 1994. 404–420.

Glennon, Daniel and Jim Jenks. *National Park Service, Underground Railroad Initiative.* <http://www.cr.nps.gov/ugrr/learn_a4.htm>.

Greenberg, Edward S. "Introduction: Models of the Political Process: Implications for the Black Community," in *Black Politics: The Inevitability of Conflict/ Readings,* New York. Holt, Rinehart and Winston, Inc., 1971. 5.

Greenlee, Sam. *The Spook Who Sat By the Door.* Detroit: Wayne State University, 1969.

Hall, Raymond. *Black Separatism in the United States.* Hanover, N.H.: UP of New England, 1978.

Hampton, Fred. "Black Panther Party Chairman Fred Hampton Speaks at University of Chicago, Parts 1&2." April 1, 1969. Freedom is a Constant Struggle Archives. San Francisco, CA. Accessed Spring 2003.

Hopkins, Pauline. *The Magazine Novels of Pauline Hopkins.* New York: Oxford UP, 1988.

Hudson-Weems, Clenora. *Africana Womanism: Reclaiming Ourselves.* Troy, MI: Bedford Publishers, 1995.

Hull, Gloria. "What it is I think She's Doing Anyhow: A Reading of Toni Cade Bambara's *The Salt Eaters* in *Home Girls: A Black Feminist Anthology*, Ed. Barbara Smith. New York: Kitchen Table: Women of Color Press. 1983. 124–141.

Hurston, Zora Neale. *Their Eyes Were Watching God*. 1937. New York: Negro UP, 1969.

Hutcheon, Linda. *The Politics of Postmodernism*. New York: Routledge, 1989.

James, Joy. *The Black Feminist Reader.* Malden, MA: Blackwell Publishers, 2000.

Jones, Leroi and Larry Neal, Eds. *Black Fire: An Anthology of Afro-American Writing*. New York: Morrow, 1968.

Jordan, Winthrop. *White Over Black: American Attitudes Toward the Negro, 1550–1812*. Baltimore: Penguin Books, Inc., 1968.

Karenga, Maulana. *Introduction to Black Studies*. Los Angeles: Kawaida, 1982.

Karenga, Ron. "Black Cultural Nationalism." *The Black Aesthetic*. Ed. Addison Gayle, Jr. Garden City: Doubleday, 1971.

Kelly, Robin. *Freedom Dreams: The Black Radical Imagination*. Boston: Beacon Press, 2002.

Kincaid, Jamaica. *A Small Place*. New York: Penguin, 1989.

King, Martin Luther. *Where Do We Go From Here: Chaos or Community?* New York: Harper & Row, 1967.

Kurlansky, Mark. *A Continent of Islands: Searching for the Caribbean Destiny*. Reading, Maine: Addison-Wesley, 1992. 24.

Lee, Valerie. *Granny Midwives and Black Women Writers: Double-Dutched Readings*. New York: Routledge, 1996. 112–122.

Levenstein, Lisa. "From Innocent Children to Unwanted Migrants and Unwed Moms: Two Chapters in the Public Discourse on Welfare in the United States, 1960- 1961." *Journal of Women's History* 11.1 3 Aug. 2004 <http://iupjournals.org/jwh/jwh11–4.html>.

Lomax, Pearl Cleage. *We Don't Need No Music*. Broadside Press: 1972.

Marable, Manning. *Black Liberation in Conservative America*. Boston: South End, 1997.

Marshall, Paule. *The Chosen Place, The Timeless People*. 1969. New York: Vintage Books, 1984.

Marx, Karl. *The Communist Manifesto*. 1872. New York: Brussel & Brussel, 1967.

Matthews, Tracye A. "No One Ever Asks What A Man's Role in the Revolution Is": Gender Politics and Leadership in the Black Panther Party, 1966–71. *Sisters in the Struggle: African American Women in the Civil Rights-Black Power Movement*. Ed. Bettye Collier-Thomas and V.P. Franklin. New York: New York UP, 2001.

McAdam, Doug. *Political Process and the Development of Black Insurgency, 1930 -1970*. Chicago : U of Chicago P, 1982.

Morris, Aldon D. *The Origins of the Civil Rights Movement*. New York: The Free Press, 1984.

Morrison, Toni. "Rootedness: The Ancestor as Foundation." *The Woman That I Am: The Literature and Culture of Contemporary Women of Color*. Ed. D. Soyini Madison. New York: St. Martin's Press, 1994. 492–297.

———. *Song of Solomon*. New York: Knopf, 1977.

National Park Service. "In Search of Freedom." http://www.cr.nps.gov/delta/underground/free.htm. Accessed 2004.

Nelson, Britta. "Ella Baker—A Leader Behind the Scenes." *FOCUS* Aug. 1993.

Nfah-Abbenyi, Juliana Makuchi. *Gender in African Women's Writing: Identity, Sexuality, and Difference*. Bloomington: Indiana University Press, 1997. 16–34.

Ogundipe-Leslie, Molara. *Re-Creating Ourselves: African Women and Critical Transformations*. Trenton: Africa World Press, Inc., 1994.

Parmar, Pratihba. "A Place of Rage." New York, NY: Women Make Movies, 1991.

Petry, Ann. *The Street*. New York: Houghton Mifflin Company, 1946.

Piven, Frances Foxand Richard A. Cloward. *Poor Peoples Movements: Why They Succeed, How They Fail*. New York: Pantheon Books, 1977.

Reagon, Bernice Johnson. "Women as Culture Carriers in the Civil Rights Movement: Fannie Lou Hamer." *Women in the Civil Rights Movement: Trailblazers and Torchbearers, 1941–1965*. Eds. Vicki L. Crawford, Jacqueline Anne Rouse, et. al. Brooklyn: Carlson Publishing, 1990.

Reid, Inez Smith. *"Together" Black Women*. New York: Emerson Hall, 1972.

Robinson, Dean. *Black Nationalism in American Politics and Thought*. New York: Cambridge UP, 2001.

Robinson, Pat. "Poor Black Women's Study papers by Poor Black Women of Mount Vernon, New York." *The Black Woman: An Anthology*. Ed. Toni Cade. New York: New American Library, 1970.

Robinson, Patricia. *Poor Black Women* Boston: New England Free Press, N.D. <http://scriptorium.lib.duke.edu/wlm/poor/>

Schuyler, George Samuel. "The Negro Art Hokum." *The Norton Anthology of African American Literature*. Eds. Henry Louis Gates, Jr., Nellie McKay, et al. New York: W.W. Norton & Co., 1997.

Shakur, Assata. "A Message to My Sistas." Letter. March 11, 2005. http://www.assatashakur.org/sistas.htm

Snail, Mgebwi Lavin. *The Antecedens (sic) and the Emergence of the Black Consciousness Movement in South Africa*. München: Akademischer Verlag, 1993.

Spriggs, Edward S. "For the TRUTH (because it is necessary) in *Black Fire: An Anthology of Afro-American Writing*. Ed. Leroi Jones and Larry Neal. New York: Morrow, 1968. 339–340.

Stewart, Maria. "On African Rights and Liberty." (1833) *Civil Rights Since 1787: A Reader on the Black Struggle*. Eds. Jonathan Birnbaum and Clarence Taylor. New York: NYU, 2000.

Styron, William. *The Confessions of Nat Turner*. New York: Random House, 1967.

Taylor, J. Douglas Allen "Septima Clark: Teacher to a Movement." Unpublished paper. 16 May 2004 <http://www.thestateonline.com/civilrights/biopage.php.>

Upton, James. Lecture. The Ohio State University, Columbus. 7 April. 2004.

Van Deburg, William. *New Day in Babylon: The Black Power Movement and American Culture, 1965–1975*. Chicago: U of Chicago P, 1992.

Walker, David. *David Walker's Appeal to the Coloured Citizens Around the World.* 1829. University Park: Pennsylvania State UP, 2000.

Wagstaff, Thomas. *Black Power: The Radical Response to White America.* Beverly Hills: Glencoe Press, 1969.

Wallace, Michelle. *Black Macho and the Myth of the Superwoman.* New York: Dial Press, 1979.

Walker, Alice. *Meridian.* New York: Harcourt Brace Jovanovich, 1976.

———. *In Search of Our Mother's Gardens: Womanist Prose.* New York: Harcourt, 1984.

Walker, Melissa. Down from the Mountaintop: Black Women's Novels in the Wake of the Civil Rights Movement. New Haven: Yale UP, 1991.

Washington, Mary Helen, "Foreword." *Their Eyes Were Watching God* by Zora Neale Hurston. New York: Harper and Row, 1990. Reprint. VII–XIV.

Wideman, John Edgar. *The Lynchers.* New York: Harcourt Brace Jovanovich, 1973.

Wilentz, Gay. *Healing Narratives: Women Writers Curing Cultural Dis-Ease.* New Brunswick: Rutgers UP, 2000.

Wright, Richard. "Blueprint for Negro Writing." *The Portable Harlem Renaissance Reader.* New York: Viking, 1994.

Wright, Richard. *Native Son.* New York: Perennial Library, 1966.

Index